C. CHRISTOPHER SMITH
AND JOHN PATTISON

SLOW CHURCH

CULTIVATING COMMUNITY
IN THE PATIENT WAY OF
JESUS

Foreword by JONATHAN WILSON-HARTGROVE

IVP Books

An imprint of InterVarsity Press
Downers Grove, Illinois

InterVarsity Press
P.O. Box 1400, Downers Grove, IL 60515-1426
World Wide Web: www.ivpress.com
Email: email@ivpress.com

InterVarsity Press® is the book-publishing division of InterVarsity Christian Fellowship/USA®, a
movement of students and faculty active on campus at hundreds of universities, colleges and schools of
nursing in the United States of America, and a member movement of the International Fellowship of
Evangelical Students. For information about local and regional activities, write Public Relations Dept.,
InterVarsity Christian Fellowship/USA, 6400 Schroeder Rd., P.O. Box 7895, Madison, WI 53707-7895,
or visit the IVCF website at www.intervarsity.org.

Cover design: David Fassett
Interior design: Beth Hagenberg
Cover Images: brick wall: jimss/Getty Images
                    ivy: © Praiwun/iStockphoto

ISBN 978-0-8308-4114-1 (print)
ISBN 978-0-8308-9595-3 (digital)

Printed in the United States of America ∞

g green
press
INITIATIVE
As a member of the Green Press Initiative, InterVarsity Press is committed to protecting
the environment and to the responsible use of natural resources. To learn more, visit
greenpressinitiative.org.

Library of Congress Cataloging-in-Publication Data

Smith, C. Christopher.
  Slow church : cultivating community in the patient way of Jesus / C.
Christopher Smith, John Pattison.
     pages cm
  Includes bibliographical references.
  ISBN 978-0-8308-4114-1 (pbk. : alk. paper)
  1. Communities—Religious aspects--Christianity. 2. Church. I. Title.
BV4517.5.S63 2014
253—dc23
                                                                                    2014011067

| P | 17 | 16 | 15 | 14 | 13 | 12 | 11 | 10 | 9 | 8 | 7 | 6 | | | | |
| Y | 28 | 27 | 26 | 25 | 24 | 23 | 22 | 21 | 20 | 19 | 18 | 17 | 16 | 15 | 14 |

For my sisters and brothers
at Englewood Christian Church,
my slow church community.

C. S.

For Kate, Molly and Julia—
my original intentional community.
And for Dave, with gratitude for two
decades of the best friendship.

J. P.

Contents

Foreword

Not long ago I was talking with a journalist about religious movements and my hope for the future of faith in North America. "You know," I said, "the movement that grabs my attention is really pretty small—a dozen or so folks at its core, most of them not spectacular. Only one of them is published. A few of them used to have good reason to kill one another. But somehow they've stayed together. And this new life they've found with one another is so important to them that they are, to a person, willing to die for it."

A good reporter, ever eager for a good lead, this fellow asked where he could learn more about this movement. "Oh, it's well known," I said. "The best-selling book of all time has four accounts of its origins—Matthew, Mark, Luke and John."

"Yes," he said matter-of-factly, "but where can I find this movement today?"

This, it seems to me, is someone asking the right question.

The book you're holding in your hands is not so ambitious as to claim that it holds the key to the future of the church in North America. But *Slow Church* is a book that's asking the right question. As its authors suggest, this book is an invitation into the long, rich, deep and necessarily *slow* conversation about what it means to be part of the movement that Jesus started two thousand years ago.

It is, in short, the sort of invitation you should neither ignore nor turn down.

"Taste and see," the authors say, echoing the psalmist. Indeed. A banquet has been prepared for you. Pull up a seat. And, while you're at it, text your friend and tell her she's invited too. This is a conversation that only gets richer as new friends come one by one to enjoy.

There's much I like about this book. Its central metaphor of the welcome table echoes the God Movement from first-century Eucharists down to the twentieth-century lunch counters. I love the way Chris and John pay attention to what God is up to beyond the church in ways that build up the church. (*Slow Church* draws on the Slow Food Movement, as well as insights from asset-based community developers, poets and social entrepreneurs.) And I'm just tickled by the delight of two amateurs in the truest sense—regular folk whose passion inspires them to reach far and wide for resources to guide a conversation about what it means to live faithfully in the way of Jesus.

But what I love most about *Slow Church* is the way this book talks about faith—and invites us to talk about it—with attention to the Word made flesh. There are some beautiful words in this book, which you will enjoy, no doubt. But rather than drawing our attention to their words, Chris and John introduce us to real communities where people like you and me are living into the ways of the Word made flesh.

Much of North American Christianity has celebrated the words of those who proclaim the gospel. But the Bible says, "How beautiful are the *feet* of those who proclaim good news."

Yes, their words are good. But here are two brothers with some beautiful feet.

Listen to them. Talk back. But most of all, follow them as they follow Christ.

Jonathan Wilson-Hartgrove
Epiphany 2014

Introduction

Above all, trust in the slow work of God,
our loving vine-dresser.

Pierre Teilhard de Chardin

A tale of two manifestoes:

In February 1909, a thirty-two-year-old Italian writer named Filippo Tommaso Marinetti caused an international stir when he published, in the French newspaper *Le Figaro,* "The Foundation and Manifesto of Futurism."

The Futurist Manifesto exalted the future over the past, violence and aggression over peace and patience, immorality over morality, men over women, the young over the old, the machine over the land, and the known over the unknown. "We will sing of great crowds excited by work, by pleasure, and by riot," Marinetti wrote; "we will sing of the multicolored, polyphonic tides of revolution in the modern capitals." Museums and libraries were to be demolished. War was the cleansing of the world. And Marinetti declared that the world's splendor had been "enriched" by a new beauty: speed. "Time and Space died yesterday. We already live in the absolute, because we have created eternal, omnipresent speed."

The Futurist Manifesto was grotesque and fascist, but in many ways it got what it called for.[1] The twentieth century turned out to be the bloodiest, most cacophonous in human history. It was a century in which our eagerness to destroy each other and plunder the planet was outstripped only by the technological advances to do them more completely. Above all, there was speed, which irrevocably reshaped society with fast cars, fast food, fast computers and "the fast track."

Eighty years after the publication of the Futurist Manifesto, another international movement with Italian roots was launched in Paris. The Slow Food Manifesto, signed in December 1989 by delegates from fifteen countries, starts: "Our century, which began and has developed under the insignia of industrial civilization, first invented the machine and then took it as its life model."[2]

The International Slow Food Movement was formed as an act of resistance against fast life and the homogenizing effects of globalization—what Alice Waters, the executive chef and co-creator of Chez Panisse restaurant calls "global standardization"—and the attendant loss of natural and cultural diversity. The name "Slow Food" was inspired by a rally against the opening of a McDonald's near the Spanish Steps in Rome. Carlo Petrini, the journalist who cofounded Slow Food, helped organize the demonstration, during which the crowd chanted, "We don't want fast food! We want slow food!" The weapons of protest that day were bowls of penne pasta.

Today, Slow Food is comprised of 1,300 local chapters and 100,000 members in fifty-three countries. Each chapter is dedicated to protecting local food and wine producers, preserving food traditions, and promoting the pleasures of conviviality—a lovely word derived from the Latin word for feast, *convivia*, literally "to live with," that implies an atmosphere of festivity. (Local Slow Food chapters are called *convivia*.)

Slow Food has inspired other Slow campaigns. Cittaslow (Slow Cities) was launched by a group of Italian mayors in October 1999 and now includes more than 140 communities in twenty-three countries. Eligible Slow Cities must have populations under 50,000 and are evaluated in the categories of sustainable agriculture, local food cultivation, land use and hospitality, among others. "These cities have decided to bet on values that thwart alienation," Cittaslow chairman Pier Giorgio Oliveti has said. "We want to limit the spread of 'non-places.'"

In 2008, the venture capitalist and entrepreneur Woody Tasch founded Slow Money with the goal of getting a million Americans to invest 1 percent of their assets in local food systems within a decade. Other manifestations include Slow Gardening, Slow Parenting, Slow Reading, Slow Design and Slow Art. There is even a World Slow Day, which some playful Italians recently celebrated by offering free public transportation, poetry contests, and free yoga and Tai Chi lessons, and by issuing fake citations to pedestrians who were walking too fast or taking too direct a route.

While these efforts differ in scope, scale and strategy, they have much in common, most obviously their opposition to what the Canadian journalist Carl Honoré describes as "the cult of speed." Fast and slow, writes Honoré, are not just rates of change. "They are shorthand for ways of being, or philosophies of life. Fast is busy, controlling, aggressive, hurried, analytical, stressed, superficial, impatient, active, quantity-over-quality. Slow is the opposite: calm, careful, receptive, still, intuitive, unhurried, patient, reflective, quality-over-quantity. It is about making real and meaningful connections—with people, culture, work, food, everything."[3]

FAST CHURCH

For better and for worse, the North American church seems to be just as susceptible as the rest of culture to the allure of fast life, or what the sociologist George Ritzer has termed "McDonaldization"— that is, "the process by which the principles of the fast-food restaurant are coming to dominate more and more sectors of American society as well as the rest of the world."[4]

Ritzer identified four dimensions of McDonaldization: efficiency, predictability, calculability (quantifiable results) and control—or at least the illusion of control. These trends, which have been at play since the dawn of the Industrial Revolution, have shaped nearly all aspects of culture, including the Western church. Western Christianity's symbiotic relationship with industrialization has led to attempts to circumvent the messy or inefficient facets of faith. Many churches, particularly those driven by church growth models, come dangerously close to reducing Christianity to a commodity that can be packaged, marketed and sold. Instead of cultivating a deep, holistic discipleship that touches every aspect of our lives, we've confined the life of faith to Sunday mornings, where it can be kept safe and predictable, or to a "personal relationship with Jesus Christ," which can be managed from the privacy of our own home. Following Jesus has been diminished to a privatized faith rather than a lifelong apprenticeship undertaken in the context of Christian community.

The industrialization of the church has, significantly, paralleled the industrialization of agriculture and the near demise of the family farm. Joel Salatin—the self-described "Christian-conservative-libertarian-environmentalist-lunatic farmer" featured in Michael Pollan's *The Omnivore's Dilemma* and the documentary *Food, Inc.*— has written that conventional agriculture experts view the soil as merely a convenient way to hold up the plant while it is fed from the top in the form of ever-increasing doses of chemical fertilizers. He describes this process as superimposing a mechanistic mindset onto a biological world. Nature, in contrast, feeds the plants from the bottom up, through the soil. Thus, for the conscientious farmer, the health of the soil is a top priority.[5]

Western Christianity has similarly adopted shortcuts that are the church equivalent of imposing a mechanistic mindset onto a biological world. When evaluated in terms of efficiency—defined as the easiest way to get someone from here to there, from unsaved to saved, from unchurched to churched—these top-down inputs seem to yield impressive short-term results: they can sometimes pack the pews. So on the upside, the church has been busy.

On the downside, it's not clear at what long-term costs these methods have been employed or how helpful and sustainable they will be going forward. Plug-and-play ministries, target marketing, celebrity pastors, tightly scripted worship performances, corporate branding, the substitution of nonhuman technology for human work, church growth formulas that can be applied without deference to local context, and programs upon programs upon programs—these entice us with promises of miraculous results in just a few easy steps. But, as evidenced by the growth of the Slow movement, Americans seem increasingly wary of being sold another product so scrubbed and polished and unsurprising you'd never guess it had been born of soil and sun and scat.

SLOW CHURCH

Slow Food and the other Slow movements hold important lessons for the American church. They compel us to ask ourselves tough questions about the ground our faith communities have ceded to the cult of speed. And they invite all of us—clergy, theologians and laypeople—to start exploring and experimenting with the possibilities of Slow Church. Not as another growth strategy, but as a way of reimagining what it means to be communities of believers gathered and rooted in particular places at a particular time.

Slow Church is inspired by the language and philosophy of the Slow Food Movement as a means to rethink the ways in which we share life together in our church communities. Just as Slow Food offers a pointed critique of industrialized food cultures and agricultures, Slow Church can help us unmask and repent of our industrialized and McDonaldized approaches to church. It can also spur our imaginations with a rich vision of the holistic, interconnected and abundant life together to which God has called us in Christ Jesus. The Slow Food Movement is fundamentally about the richness of a common life with the neighbors who grow our food, prepare our food and share our food. Slow Church is a call for intentionality, an awareness of our mutual interdependence with all people and all creation, and an attentiveness to the world around us and the work God is doing in our very own neighborhoods.

Is it time for a Slow Church manifesto? Maybe not. But our goal for this book (and our blog at slowchurch.com) is to help inaugurate what we hope is a broad and long and even *slow* conversation on the topic. By necessity, the conversation will have to include issues of justice, manageable scale, diversity, seasonality (relating to both the liturgical calendar and the life and death of individual faith communities), pleasure, beauty, risk, place, time, common space and shared traditions. Limited space means that this book will touch on all these points but rigorously unpack just a few.

The principles of the Slow Food movement are *good, clean* and *fair*. We've reimagined them here as *ethics, ecology* and *economy*. By ethics we mean an allegiance to quality as opposed to quantity or efficiency. The ethics of Slow Church is the challenge to be, faithfully and well, the embodiment of Christ in a particular place. By ecology we mean that our call to follow Christ must be understood within God's mission of the reconciliation of all things. This compels us to pay more attention to not only *what* we are pursuing as churches, but *how* we do so. Economy refers to God's abundant provision for God's reconciling work.

In keeping with our slow theme, we have structured this book as a three-course meal, with the caveat that you can't talk about one course of Slow Church without talking about all the others. The courses of this meal might be brought out one after the other, but they are all eaten together, and their tastes mingle on our tongues and gradually energize our church communities. Our "meal" is preceded by a brief overview of the theology of Slow Church. And it culminates in a chapter on what we think may be the most important practice of Slow Church: conversation. We need to learn how to talk to each other.

To that end, each chapter includes conversation starters—not unlike the queries Quakers use as prompts for meditation—to help start discussion.

THE PLACES WE INHABIT

Before we go any further, we want to briefly describe our particular places, our *terroir,* the very different contexts in which we live and work and write this book.

John is in the mid–Willamette River Valley in western Oregon. For several years, John and his wife lived in Portland, where they helped start a house church that came to be known as Family Dinner. But John and his wife felt called to country life. They now live with their young daughter in rural Marion County, in a town called Silverton, where they are members of an evangelical Quaker meeting.

Silverton is surrounded by nurseries, Christmas tree farms, filbert orchards, hops fields, and fields of marionberries, blueberries and seed crops. The town is quaint and a little eccentric. It is also tough to pin down politically. Silverton's recent voting pattern is 48.52 percent Democrat and 48.79 percent Republican. The town is represented by a Democrat in the US House of Representatives and two Republicans in the state legislature. Its mayor is the first openly transgender mayor in the country.

The town doesn't conform to many trends of rural communities. Silverton is getting younger, not older, and the median age is a surprisingly low thirty-five years old. Many rural towns are slowly dying, especially as young people relocate to the big city after high school and college. Silverton, in contrast, is growing. Fast. This comes with its own set of challenges, of course. Old-timers see the town changing before their eyes. There is a legitimate concern that if Silverton becomes a "bedroom community," a place where people sleep between commutes to and from Salem and Portland, it might forget its history or lose its essential character. (As this book goes to print, a group John helped found in Silverton, the Upstream Makers Collective, is designing a project that will start collecting oral histories and presenting them back to the community in the form of stories, short plays, mini-documentaries and visual art.)

Part of what makes Silverton so lovely is that from the beginning it was designed with deference to the local landscape, including Silver Creek, which runs through the center of town.[6] Though Silverton is growing outward (there are now several subdivisions), it takes seriously its connection to the land. Silverton is the home to the Oregon Garden. It is also the "gateway" to Silver Falls State Park, which boasts fourteen waterfalls. The local granges were at one time a focal point of local farming life, but membership has dwindled in recent years. John is working with several local groups—including advocates for agriculture, the arts and cycling—to consider the role of a country grange in an age of rural flight, farm consolidation and hypermobility.

Chris, his wife Jeni, and their three children are part of the Englewood Christian Church community in Indianapolis. Their church has been in the same location in the Englewood neighborhood for over 118 years. Englewood is a tiny postage stamp of a neighborhood, consisting of about twelve blocks, one of about twenty such neighborhoods that make up Indy's Near Eastside. Chris's neighborhood has a rich history: At the turn of the twentieth century, Englewood was home to the first professional baseball stadium in Indianapolis, on a location that would later house an amusement park called Wonderland. For most of its history, Englewood was sandwiched between two major industrial complexes—RCA to the north, where all kinds of electronics were manufactured and where RCA records were pressed (including many of Elvis Presley's later albums), and, to the south, the P. R.

Mallory company, a metallurgy specialist that developed and branded the Duracell battery in the 1960s. Both manufacturing complexes were closed in the 1990s.

Englewood Christian Church—an Independent Christian Church in the Stone-Campbell tradition—began in 1895 and existed for the first half of its history as a neighborhood church, but in the 1960s and early 1970s it grew into a megachurch of more than two thousand members (though attendance on any given Sunday was significantly smaller). The pastor who had energized much of that growth left in the mid-1970s, and the size of the congregation plummeted for about a decade. For the last twenty-five years the church has immersed itself in exploring what it means to be fully present in its neighborhood.

Though the Englewood neighborhood faces many challenges common to abandoned urban communities—including drugs and prostitution—it is a place with many assets: its own public library branch, sturdy housing stock, a community garden, thoughtful and colorful murals, and above all, wonderful neighbors. About three-quarters of the church congregation lives in or just outside the Englewood neighborhood, including fifteen households on Chris's block on Oxford Street. Over the last decade a wave of Spanish-speakers have moved into the neighborhood, bringing with them new businesses like a grocery store and a tamale shop.

Englewood is a gritty, urban neighborhood. Chris and his family love being there, mostly for the people but also for the transformation God is working in their own hearts, in the hearts of their neighbors and in the place as a whole.

A NEW SHARED STORY

Although we live in strikingly different neighborhoods, one thing we have in common is our love for the church. Very early in the writing process, when the book you have in your hands was little more than a gleam in its authors' eyes, it was twice suggested to us (very politely, we hasten to add) that a book about Slow Church should be written by a specialist.

It's true that we aren't vocational pastors, expert theologians or professional church planters. In fact, we are proud *amateurs*—but in the older, more interesting sense of that word. The word *amateur* is most commonly used today to mean (a) someone who engages in a pursuit on an unpaid basis, (b) someone who is "contemptibly inept" at an activity or (c) both. But *amateur* comes to us from the French and it literally means "lover." It implies a passionate love for the thing itself, quite separate from any compensation (money, fame, career) that could come from it.[7]

Slow Food wasn't started by farmers. It was started by eaters who stood up and declared that they were no longer content to be passive consumers of industrialized food. Thus, we think it's appropriate that a lot of the energy in the early stages of the Slow Church conversation comes from nonspecialists who are motivated by a love of God, a love for the body of Christ in the world, and a desire to be more than passive consumers of religious goods and services. We want more risk, beauty and wonder than can be experienced at a spiritual filling station. We want some skin in the game.

"Eating is an agricultural act," Wendell Berry famously said, and Slow Food views consumers as active participants in the production process.[8] Eaters who know where their food comes from, know how it got to their table and support local farmers become nothing less than coproducers.

Similarly, Slow Church is more than a consumerist experience. It goes beyond just offering people a safe haven on Sunday morning from the storms of fast life. Slow Church is a way of being authentically connected as coproducers to a Story that is as big as the planet (bigger) and as intimate as our own backyards.

1

A Theological Vision
for Slow Church

We are impatient, anxious to see the whole picture,
but God lets us see things slowly, quietly.
The Church [has] to learn how to wait.

Pope Francis

🍂

One modern poet described clichés as "poetry that won." Is there any better example of that than these famous lines from William Shakespeare's play *As You Like It?* "All the world's a stage / And all the men and women merely players / They have their exits and their entrances." This trope has become so familiar that we can lose sight of the profound truths it contains. But this metaphor— the world as a singular drama in which all creation is engaged—is foundational to the theology of Slow Church.

To say that creation is a drama is to imply that it is an *enactment,* a combination of saying and doing that encompasses God, humanity and even nonhumanity (the creaturely world). As Kevin Vanhoozer has written, in the drama of creation, "God and humanity are alternately actor and audience. Better: life is human-divine interactive theatre, and theology involves both what God has said and done for the world and what we must say and do in grateful response."[1]

The biblical narrative is the story of the whole creation, from the beginning through the present to the end—and yet it's not so much a script that we mechanically act out but rather a story that serves to form us into the people we need to be. The dramas we're most familiar with, on stage or screen, are based on scripts that tell actors what to say and do. But there is another kind of drama—improvisation.

Improvisation is based on the spontaneous interactions between the players. Though all scripted dramas leave some room for the unscripted, in improv, actors are given only a scenario, a basic plotline or a few props as a starting point from which to construct a scene and enact a story. Improv can be gut-bustingly funny or painfully awkward, but either way, one can never tell the turns it will take or where it will end up.

In her memoir *Bossypants,* the comedian and writer Tina Fey talks about "the rules of improvisation that will change your life and reduce belly fat." Her first rule of improvisation is to always agree with your improv partner. The second rule of improv is to say not just yes but "YES, AND." "It's your responsibility to contribute," Fey writes. "Always make sure you're adding something to the discussion. Your initiations are worthwhile." Reflecting on Scripture as improv, Fey's words remind us that no one is a passive observer in the biblical drama. Later, Fey gives another rule of improv: "THERE ARE NO MISTAKES, only opportunities," which could be reappropriated theologically as an allusion to God's eschatological reconciliation of all things.[2]

Scripture is less like the movie of the week and more like improvisation. It provides a basic plotline and then gives our churches, the actors in this drama, extraordinary freedom and creative opportunity. In his book *Scripture and the Authority of God,* N. T. Wright describes the history of creation as a drama in five acts:

Act One: Creation

Act Two: The Fall

Act Three: Israel

Act Four: Jesus

Act Five: The Church

The implications of this are profound, if for no other reason than that it undermines our cultural impulse to be consumers and spectators rather than faithful participants in the unwritten fifth act of God's play. Wright says, "We must act in an appropriate manner for this moment in the story; this will be in direct continuity with the previous acts (we are not free to jump suddenly to another narrative, a different play altogether), but such continuity also implies discontinuity, a moment where genuinely new things can and do happen."[3]

The enactment of Scripture has astonishing formative power. The deeper our engagement with the story, the better our improvisation will be. "Improvisation in the theatre," says pastor and theologian Sam Wells, "is a practice through which actors develop trust in themselves and one another in order that they may conduct unscripted dramas without fear."[4] Similarly, Wells says that it is within the people of God—a community of trust—that we learn to live into the looming unknown of the future. The people of God are thus a sort of acting troupe that is attentive to and engaged with the scriptural story, for the purposes of building trust and learning to improvise the scriptural plotline more faithfully in the future.

THE PATIENT CHARACTER OF GOD

All around us we see the "huge spontaneous upheaval of the entire human race" that Thomas Merton talked about, a revolution he rightly predicted would be manifested in desperation, cynicism, violence, self-contradiction, fear and hope, doubt and belief, creation and destruction, and "obsessive attachments to images, idols, slogans, programs that only dull the general anguish for a moment until it bursts out everywhere."[5] In the midst of the frantic, churning, disturbed and roiling shallow waters of postmodernity, Slow

Church seeks to anchor itself in the deep, still waters of a remarkably patient yet radically immanent God. This isn't escapism. Rather, it is part and parcel of living as the peculiar people of God. As someone once said, we're *in* the world but not *of* the world, so we can be *for* the world.

In everything, Slow Church looks ahead to the eschatological redemption that is the climax of the central drama of the world. Slow Church takes the long view, examining all thought and culture, every ideology and assumption, all action and reaction by the messianic light of the last day.[6] Paradoxically, taking the long view allows us to be truly attentive to the details of the here and now. It all matters. Nothing is wasted.

Scripture illuminates characteristics of both God's nature and human nature that contribute to the slowness of our enacting of the scriptural story together. Let's consider first the nature of God.

God is transforming and reconciling the world. But unlike human revolutionaries who demand instant and total change, God is not impatient. The arc of the universe bends toward the full reconciliation of all creation, but—"Come, Lord Jesus!"—that arc is long. Jesus' parables in Matthew 13 of the leavened dough and the mustard seed remind us that God's transformation comes slowly, working outward from the place where the change begins. In an age when instant gratification reigns supreme, the lesson of these parables is provocative and surprisingly insistent—but this seems to be the way God usually works in the world. As A.W. Tozer said, "The faith of Christ offers no button to push for quick service. The new order must wait the Lord's own time."

God's patience flows from God's love for creation. It's no accident that the first characteristic of love Paul mentions in 1 Corinthians 13 is patience. Indeed, since the earliest years of the church, many important theologians—including Tertullian and Origen—have reframed the biblical story through the lens of the patience of God. Adam and Eve sinned brashly, but God was patient. For centuries,

God waited out the rebellion of humanity before calling Abraham and beginning in him the work of gathering a set-apart people. God tarried for forty years with the Israelites in the wilderness before leading them into the Promised Land. God patiently waited through the era of Israel's many kings—some rebellious against God, others less so—and sent prophets to redirect people back to God and God's unfolding story. Though we tend to gloss over it in our anticipation of the birth of Christ, the genealogy of Jesus in Matthew 1 is a testimony to God's patient communion with the people of God. And the history of the church is marked by many of the same characteristics as the history of Israel: lots of human rebellion, scattered pockets of human faithfulness, and all the while, God's deep and unwavering patience.

When church fathers like Tertullian spoke of God's patience using the Latin word *patientia,* they had in mind something more than just waiting, the way we typically understand patience today. Their use of this word is more akin to the term "longsuffering" used by translators of the King James Version in verses like Numbers 14:18 ("The Lord is longsuffering, and of great mercy, forgiving iniquity and transgression") and when describing the fruits of the Spirit in Galatians 5:22. God is ever faithful to the divine nature and mission in the world, even preferring to be humiliated and to suffer than to deviate from the work of love and reconciliation. This longsuffering is best exemplified for us in the earthly ministry of Jesus from beginning (his temptations in the wilderness) to end (his arrest and crucifixion). The character of God thus stands in sharp contrast to the modern era's idolatrous affair with efficiency, which is driven by the conviction that the end justifies the means—or, in the famous words of Malcolm X, that some vital ends should be pursued "by any means necessary."

We'll explore the concept of *patientia* in more depth in chapter four. For now, though, as we begin to reflect on the slowness of God's work in the world, it's important to be mindful that our calling into the abundant life of Slow Church begins with the love, patience and longsuffering of God.

GOD DESIRES COLLABORATION WITH HUMANITY

In sharp contrast to an earthly tyrant who brutalizes his subjects into fearful submission, God lovingly and patiently involves humanity in the work of reconciliation. This desire for collaboration is the second aspect of God's character that contributes to the slowness (and goodness) of the redemption story. The tiniest actions of human faithfulness to God's mission are slowly and patiently woven together into the great biblical drama of reconciliation. God desires the radical transformation of our broken world, but unlike human revolutionaries who, in their impatience, resort to violence toward humanity and creation, God isn't short on time. And, as we will see, God works with humanity even in our shortsightedness and rebellion.

God's patient collaboration with humankind is evident throughout the biblical story, even when such collaboration appears at face value to be at cross-purposes with the mission of reconciliation. We see this when the people of Israel begged God to give them a king (1 Sam 8). Israel's pagan neighbors had kings. God made it clear that having a king wasn't in Israel's best interests, that a monarch would dominate the people, conscript their sons for war and their daughters for household service, and take the best of their fields and orchards and vineyards. The Israelites persisted and God relented. God was right, of course, about the way many of Israel's kings would abuse their people, and yet it would be the "Lion of the tribe of Judah" and the "Root of David" that would ransom "for God saints from every tribe and language and people and nation" (Rev 5:1-10). What's more, we all condemned Jesus to death and crucified him, but even there God was at work, engaging humanity with the power of resurrection.

God's plan has always been centered on the gathering of a peculiar people who will embody God's reconciliation. God's collaboration with humanity is therefore located primarily, though not exclusively, in the people of God. To return to our world-stage metaphor, the primary players in this drama are God and the troupe of actors we call God's people. This collaboration is eloquently described by German Catholic priest and professor Gerhard Lohfink:

> God is thus revealed as omnipotent precisely in the fact that God stakes everything on the intelligence, free will, and trust of human beings. . . . God attains the goal desired because in this world joy in God's story is stronger than all inertia and greed, so that this *joy continually seizes people and gathers them into the people of God.*[7]

HUMAN NATURE AND THE SLOWNESS OF GOD'S RECONCILIATION

There are two aspects of human nature that also contribute to the slowness of God's reconciliation. The first is *human rebelliousness.* Just as the story of creation has been marked by God's constancy and patience, it's also been shot through by human sinfulness, from the disobedience of Adam and Eve onward. We believe our ideas about how things should be done are better than God's. Driven by selfishness, we are all too inclined to act upon our desires for comfort and control and self-preservation instead of following God's leading. We pretend God isn't an actor in this great drama, let alone sovereign over all of it. We ignore the integrity of God's creation. We insist on taking care of ourselves first—either as individuals or as one ethnic group, one nationality or some other subset of humanity—which ultimately leads to the dehumanization and oppression of those who aren't like us.

The primary roots of our rebellion are distrust and fear. We don't trust that God is faithful. Like Adam and Eve, we wonder if God is really in charge, if we will be taken care of or if we are being tricked. When God holds something back we're tempted to believe God is

trying to hold *us* back, as when Satan muses to himself in the
Garden in *Paradise Lost*:

> All is not theirs it seems.
> One fatal Tree there stands of Knowledge called
> Forbidden them to taste. Knowledge forbidden?
> Suspicious, reasonless. Why should their Lord
> Envy them that? Can it be sin to know?
> Can it be death? And do they only stand
> By ignorance? Is that their happy state,
> The proof of their obedience and their faith?
> O fair foundation laid whereon to build
> Their ruin![8]

As we noted earlier in Sam Wells's definition of improvisation, it is
through faithful engagement with God's people that we learn how
to play our part in the drama of redemption. Gradually we learn to
speak and act not out of fear and doubt but out of trust in God and
care for our fellow humans. One of the wonderful things about
improv is that mistakes and missteps can eventually be redeemed
if the actors are creative, committed to each other and committed
to the success of the story. Similarly, as the biblical narrative repeatedly makes clear, God's collaborative action with humanity can
eventually unravel, and even redeem, the worst consequences of
human rebellion.

THE HUMAN STRUGGLE TO DISCERN GOOD FROM EVIL

The second aspect of human nature we want to consider here is our
struggle to discern good from evil. Even when our hearts want to act
faithfully in the drama of reconciliation, it's not always clear what
the right and faithful course of action is. John Howard Yoder has
argued that as a result of the fragmentation of the Fall, humankind
can't reliably know what parts of creation reflect God's good intentions. "Of course we have access to the good creation of God," he

says. But what we don't have is "epistemologically reliable access" that permits us to know where or how to disentangle the created goodness "from the perversion and rebelliousness."[9]

We underestimate our capacity to deceive ourselves. In our fragmented state, we have lost the capacity to make ethical discernments with certainty. The reliability of our discernment improves as we reach beyond our individual selves to engage others in the discerning process, and even more so as we seek to know the way of Jesus together as God's people. But the reliability of our knowledge will never be complete until God's mission of reconciliation is finished.

God wants to work with us, but our contributions are often marred by ignorance, distrust, fear, defiance and disobedience. It's not difficult to see why the enactment of the biblical story unfolds slowly. Any argument for Fast Church, or the efficiency and expediency of Christian faithfulness, must ignore or minimize the effects of these facets of the divine and human natures.

THE PEOPLE OF GOD IN THE MISSION OF RECONCILIATION

The people of God are at the heart of God's mission for reconciling creation. In the Western world where individualism reigns supreme, there is unfamiliarity, awkwardness and even slowness in our calling to live as a community of God's people. We are so accustomed to living and acting as autonomous individuals that the idea of being God's people in the world can be tough to wrap our heads around. Being God's people is messy at best. We are broken human beings with fears, prejudices, addictions and habits that are harmful to ourselves and others. It can seem more practical and convenient (and even considerate!) to keep to ourselves and minimize the risk that we'll get entangled in the lives of others. And yet, as much as we are formed by Western individualism, and though we have allowed that individualism to shape the way we read Scripture, our calling in Christ is to *community,* to a life shared with others in a local gathering that is an expression of Christ's body in our particular place. The people of God become a sort of demonstration plot for what God intends for all humanity and all creation.

Gerhard Lohfink has argued persuasively in his books *Jesus and Community* and *Does God Need the Church?* that the community of God's people is essential to the mission of reconciliation. Lohfink emphasizes that the people of God are not privileged over the rest of humanity or the rest of creation; we are image-bearers of God, and God loves us all. But in order to redeem fallen humanity, God began the mission of reconciliation at a single time and place, and with a single people, Israel. God's work in the world is focused on gathering a people. This started with Abraham and with God's promise that Abraham's descendants would be as numerous as the stars in the sky or the grains of sand on the beach. The descendants of Abraham, Isaac and Jacob multiplied, were enslaved by Egypt, and later led out of captivity by Moses. God gave the Israelites the Torah, which wasn't primarily an instruction book for the righteous living of individuals, but laws that gave shape to a holy people, set apart from the violent, cruel and self-indulgent ways of the pagan nations that surrounded them. Israel continued to grow over the centuries, the era of kings came and went, and the life of the people of Israel fell into a pattern of occupation and exile and return.

Jesus was born in Bethlehem, the city of David, a backwater town that paradoxically confirmed Jesus's kingship, when Israel was under imperial Roman occupation. There has been a strong temptation throughout the history of the church to place Jesus over and against the work God started in Israel. This flawed theology, called *supercessionism*, fails to see the historical integrity of God's people-building work in the world. The old tree wasn't chopped down to make room for the new one; Gentile Christians were, in the words of the apostle Paul, a branch grafted onto the olive tree of Israel (Rom 11:1-24). The reconciling work of Jesus extends outward from the people of Israel.

Though he often challenged the religious and political elites of his day, Jesus was a Jew in first-century, Roman-occupied Palestine. As Lohfink observes, it is striking that Jesus' work was centered on the calling and teaching of a small community of twelve disciples. This number indicated that the mission of Jesus was oriented toward the fullness of Israel. Jesus' disciples were all Jews, but there was a wide diversity among them. Matthew the tax collector and Simon the Zealot were two disciples whose backgrounds couldn't have been more difficult to reconcile. "In a tax-collector and a Zealot the most bitterly opposed forces that existed in Israel at the time were joined within a single group," notes Lohfink, "for the tax-collectors gathered revenue for the Romans while the Zealots utterly rejected the Roman occupation as incompatible with the reign of God."[10]

Called by Christ, the disciples were a community. We tend to think of Jesus and his disciples in terms of their religious activities—for instance, preaching the good news and casting out demons—but we shouldn't forget that their common life was much broader. They ate together, traveled together and shared in all facets of life. Centered as they were on Jesus, these seemingly mundane activities took on religious significance.

Through the dispersion of the disciples after Pentecost, God's work of gathering a people was extended beyond the boundaries of Israel. Out of Israel, after many generations, a Messiah was raised up who opened the doors so that the blessings of chosenness would now be available to all, regardless of their ethnic heritage. There is a continuity to God's work in the world: the calling and shaping of a community of people that began in Israel has, through the work of Christ and the little community of his twelve disciples, been extended to Gentiles as well as Jews. "The Church did not regard itself as a *new* people appearing in the stead of the old people of God, having dissolved and replaced it," Lohfink says, "but as *Israel,* or more precisely as the beginning and center of growth for the eschatological Israel. . . . The post-Easter community continued what Jesus had begun."[11] Furthermore, if we take Ezekiel's vision of the valley of the dry bones seriously, it is not only we as individuals who have died and been resurrected in Christ, but "the whole house of Israel" (Ezek 37:11).

A DEEP-SEATED JOY

The resurrection of Jesus relieves us of the fear of death. "Where, O death, is your victory? Where, O death, is your sting?" (1 Cor 15:55). But the fuller story of the New Testament is that God's people have been resurrected as the body of Christ. Just as Jesus is the embodiment of the *shalom* that God intends for creation, the church's role in the drama of Creation is likewise to be the embodiment of God's *shalom,* albeit in a form that hasn't yet been fully realized.

At the root of the Greek word for church, *ekklesia,* is the verb meaning "to call out." We have been called out of the old creation and into a new creation characterized by abundant life. "If anyone is in Christ," Paul wrote to the Corinthian church, "there is a new creation: everything old has passed away; see, everything has become new!" (2 Cor 5:17). Thus, we see that the eternal life we have in Christ is not only everlasting temporally but also limitless in its quality. Lohfink describes this distinction:

> Those who love their sisters and brothers have already passed from death to life (I John 3:14). The border between life and death, the real threshold, is no longer physical death, but the dying that takes place in baptism. In [the text of Acts 2], this eschatological consciousness is indicated in the "gladness" or the "jubilation" by which Luke refers to the eschatological joy of the *ekklesia,* which in celebrating the breaking of bread is already sharing in heavenly joy.[12]

The hallmark of our faith is the joy we have in the resurrection life of Christ. This joy is what attracted people to the early Christian communities described in the Acts narrative, and it is joy that should make our church communities attractive to others today (Acts 2:42-47). The good news is really and truly wonderful news. It is a deep-seated joy, both now and forever.

To say the gospel is attractive is not to advocate for "church growth" or any of the ideologies of the so-called attractional churches. Michael Frost and Alan Hirsch describe *attractional* as an "approach to Christian mission in which the church develops programs, meetings, services, or other 'products' in order to attract unbelievers into the influence of the Christian community."[13] They suggest that perhaps 95 percent of Western churches operate with a "come and hear" mentality that all but requires unbelievers to enter our sanctified spaces to hear the gospel. Frost and Hirsch make a convincing case that the attractional church will be of limited effectiveness in post-Christendom, calling instead for an *incarnational* church that "disassembles itself and seeps into the cracks and crevices of a society" in order to represent Christ to the world.[14]

The primary work of Slow Church is not attracting people to our church buildings, but rather cultivating together the resurrection life of Christ, by deeply and selflessly loving our brothers and sisters, our neighbors and even our enemies. As we holistically embody Christ's love, we find joy that we pray will draw people closer to Christ. According to Frost and Hirsch, the outmoded Christendom way of thinking is attractional, dualistic and hierarchical. It is a "bounded set" and sees people as either in or out, those who belong and those who don't. It believes in good, strong fences. But as Robert Frost's poem "Mending Wall" makes clear, the inherited notion that "good fences make good neighbors" is almost always wrong:

> Before I built a wall I'd ask
> What I was walling in or walling out
> And to whom I was like to give offence
> Something there is that doesn't love a wall,
> That wants it down!

Walls, borders and clear lines of demarcation give shape to the bounded set. The incarnational church, in contrast, is a "centered set." A centered set is defined by its core values. It sees people "not . . . as in or out, but as closer or further away from the center [which in this case is Christ]. In that sense, everyone is in and no one is out. Though some people are close to the center and others far from it, everyone is potentially part of the community in its broadest sense."[15]

In one of Wendell Berry's short stories, the character Burley Coulter says: "The way we are, we are members of each other. All of us. Everything. The difference ain't in who is a member and who is not, but in who knows it and who don't."[16] To return to our stage metaphor: *all* the men and women are players, whether they know it or not. The nature of the drama being played out in creation is that the troupe of actors who were conscious of the drama and actively cooperating with it began small, but it is slowly expanding, gradually winning the trust of all humanity until everyone is playing his or her role.

At the heart of our vision of Slow Church is a theology deeply rooted in the importance of the people of God to God's mission in the world and in the rich joy of *shalom* that comes to all creation as we grow and flourish in the places to which we have been called. Over the course of the remaining chapters of this book, we will flesh out a vision of how the ethics, ecology and economy of Slow Church shed light on our calling as local faith communities and deepen our engagement together in the unfolding drama of God's reconciliation of all things.

CONVERSATION STARTERS

1. According to Scripture, what is the ultimate end to which God is bringing all of creation? What is God doing in and with the world?

2. According to Scripture, how has God chosen to accomplish

God's mission in the world? What is the role that the church has been given?

3. What are the particular strategic initiatives to which God has called our local congregation, in its particular time and place, in participation with God's mission?

4. What are the theological and practical convictions that we share as a congregation and that give shape to our following together in the way of Jesus?

5. What are our shared practices for intentionally nurturing the formation of our congregation as a local church community?

First Course

2

Terroir

Taste and See

To live within limits. To want one thing.
Or a few things very much and love them dearly.
Cling to them, survey them from every angle. Become
one with them—that is what makes the poet,
the artist, the human being.

J. W. Goethe

I (John) grew up in the Midwest. We moved around a lot for my dad's job, and I got pretty adept at making the transition from one city, one neighborhood, one school to another. The hardest move, though, was the one we made when I was in the ninth grade. We changed states—from Kansas to Nebraska—and moved from a tiny, rural town to the bustling metropolis of Lincoln. I struggled to make friends at my big new school. Eventually I fell in with the role-playing kids, but I felt like a chameleon. I didn't have any real interest in special powers and twelve-sided dice; I had just learned to blend in perfectly with my surroundings.

What saved me from disappearing altogether was the church my family came to call home. The church was big—nearly one thousand people in attendance every weekend—but we Pattisons

found our niche. Every Sunday morning, and at least twice
midweek, the family piled into our Dodge Caravan for the fifty-
minute round-trip drive from our house on 27th and J Street to the
church complex on the outskirts of town. Dad and Mom joined a
small group. The five of us boys joined Awana, youth group and
church league basketball teams. My first real girlfriends were at
that church. My best friend these last seventeen years is from that
church. When I was in high school I served as a volunteer leader
for the junior high youth group, and I loved it. The only reason
I'm on Facebook is so I can keep in touch with those junior high
kids, who are now, like me, in their thirties, many of them married
with children.

I bring all this up because I'm about to be a little critical of a
church that played a major role in shaping who I am today, a church
for which I have nothing but fond feelings.

Lincoln was the home of the University of Nebraska. A lot of
students went to our church, and after I finished high school I
started attending the church's big college group. I soon discovered
that the college group patterned itself in many ways after Willow
Creek, the megachurch in the Chicago suburbs that has an average
weekend attendance of twenty-four thousand. Willow Creek
Church is a pioneer of the hyphenated approach to church growth:
seeker-sensitive, purpose-driven, program-driven. Willow Creek's
vision of church life was heavily influenced by the principles of
business management. In fact, outside its pastor's office hung a
poster that said, "What is our business? Who is our customer?
What does the customer consider value?"[1]

In 2007, Willow Creek did a brave and humble thing. It published the results of a massive multiyear study, which found that
many of the hallmarks of their church growth strategy—some
elements of which had cost millions of dollars to implement—
weren't working. They were beefing up attendance, but they
weren't necessarily yielding spiritual growth and discipleship. But

back in the late 1990s, when I was attending this church in Lincoln, my college group leaders were regularly traveling to Willow Creek for conferences and coming home with curriculum and models and materials. What they wanted to see happen— young people coming to know Jesus—was laudable. But it felt to me like they just wanted to replicate Willow Creek's programs in Lincoln, expecting to get the same results. I couldn't explain why at the time, but there was something about all this that didn't sit right with me. It didn't seem . . . *indigenous*.

Then one night I was invited to attend a banquet for a nationally syndicated Christian talk show. One of the other guests that night was Dr. Warren Wiersbe, a well-known author and Bible teacher who went to my church. Toward the end of the banquet Dr. Wiersbe came over to the table where a friend and I were sitting. He asked us how things were going, and somehow we got on the topic of the college group. I expressed some of my frustrations about how we seemed to be just copying Willow Creek. Dr. Wiersbe said something to us that night that I never forgot, and it planted an early seed of Slow Church. He said, "Just remember, you can never franchise the blessings of God."

THE TASTE OF THE PLACE

You can't franchise the kingdom of God. Certainly there seem to be some repeatable characteristics of the kingdom. Demons are cast out. People are healed. Walls of division come tumbling down. It is good news for the poor. But we see in Jesus' description of the new wine and old wineskins in Mark 2 that it is the nature of the gospel to burst old paradigms. Elsewhere, Jesus' descriptions of the kingdom of God as being like yeast and a mustard seed imply a framework for growth that is organic, often invisible to the naked eye and ultimately mysterious.

Simon the magician tried franchising the Spirit in Acts 8, a plan for which he was firmly rebuked by Peter. We aren't accusing anyone of "simony," the ancient sin of trying to pay for power and influence in the church, but we do believe firmly that the kingdom of God isn't something that can be purchased. And yet many churches, particularly those driven by the church growth movement, come dangerously close to reducing Christianity to a commodity that can be packaged and marketed and sold.

A McDonald's or Burger King restaurant is essentially a caloric filling station. Due in large part to its high concentration of fats and sugars, fast food offers a source of cheap calories.[2] And everything about the fast food experience is designed to get people in and out as quickly as possible. The drive-through lane is being constantly rejiggered to shave seconds off a customer's experience, even to the point of creating automated welcome messages and outsourcing drive-through customer service to India. A McDonald's restaurant is designed to be uncomfortable. Its seating, lighting and color schemes are all designed to discourage people from lingering.

In the same way, a church that has given itself over to the forces of McDonaldization can become a spiritual filling station, our Sunday morning pit stop before we head back out into the rat race. Churches become dispensaries of religious goods and services, which falsely bifurcates life into the spiritual and nonspiritual. Slow Church tries to move away from this compartmentalized paradigm. The wisdom of the cross is pertinent to all aspects of life. The world is fallen, and the way God has chosen to redeem the world is place by place, gathering communities that together seek the common good, the redemption, the *shalom* of particular places.

One of the keys to understanding Slow Church is captured in the seventeenth-century French phrase *le goût de terroir,* which can be translated "the taste of the place." Carlo Petrini, the cofounder of Slow Food, writes often about *terroir* as "the combination of natural factors (soil, water, slope, height above sea level, vegetation, micro-climate) and human ones (tradition and practice and cultivation) that gives a unique character to each small agricultural locality and the food grown, raised, made, and cooked there."[3] Thus, a Pinot noir from Oregon's Willamette Valley takes on the taste and texture of the grape, the soil, the barrel and the late frost. In the same way, Slow Church is rooted in the natural, human and spiritual cultures of a particular place. It is a distinctively local expression of the global body of Christ. "The Word became flesh and blood, and moved into the neighborhood" (Jn 1:14 *The Message*).

With a commitment to place, and with gratitude for the immensity of God's gifts there, our churches become catalysts of human flourishing: nurturing local economies and local culture, and seeking the common good of our places. Slow Church is a journey in the direction of ethics, of preferring quality over quantity, of seeking the well-being of our congregation as well as our neighborhood.

In his book *Missional: Joining God in the Neighborhood,* Alan Roxburgh writes that the way to know God is to "[enter] into the ordinary, everyday life of the neighborhoods and communities where we live."[4] He says later:

I'm appealing for the recovery of local and particular ways of calling forth the personal once more in the towns and neighborhoods where we live. For me, this is about dwelling among, working beside, and eating at the table of the men and women who live in our communities, who long for the personal rather than the pitch.[5]

We are bound one to another, but a culture built on speed wants to fling us out from the center like a centrifuge. Thus, to commit ourselves to cultivating goodness through practices of nearness and stability, and to conversationally develop shared traditions, is to take a stand against alienation. It is a way of crafting a new, shared story for the community, while connecting us to the cosmic church across time and prefiguring the kingdom of God. It is also an acknowledgment that our fates are wrapped up with the fates of our neighbors. As the prophet Jeremiah wrote in his letter to the exiles,

"But seek the welfare of the city where I have sent you into exile, and pray to the LORD on its behalf, for in its welfare you will find your welfare" (Jer 29:7).

Fifteen years ago, Bruce Wilkinson published a book called *The Prayer of Jabez*, based loosely on the prayer of a man named Jabez in 1 Chronicles: "Oh that you would bless me and enlarge my border, and that your hand might be with me, and that you would keep me from hurt and harm!" (4:10). Wilkinson challenged his readers to pray the Jabez prayer for the next thirty days, promising that they would see significant changes in their life. The book sold tens of millions of copies and spawned a journal, devotional Bible, *The Prayer of Jabez for Women* and a companion CD of worship music. The book has been roundly criticized for its proximity to the false promises of the prosperity gospel. But lost in that sea of (valid) criticism is the perhaps subtler critique that in an age of consumerism, economic imperialism and what Martin Luther King Jr. called "jumboism," the sacrificial way of Jesus may be calling us to forsake the supersized life. We like the suggestion made by our friend Paul Sparks, one of the cofounders of the Parish Collective, that we pray the "reverse prayer of Jabez":

> God,
> Shrink our territory,
> And narrow our boundaries
> That we might truly be a blessing to all.[6]

THE CHURCH GROWTH MOVEMENT

Slow Church happens when people live, work, worship, go to school, eat, grow, learn, heal and play in proximity to each other, often outside the walls of the sanctuary. In contrast, the church growth movement often has little interest in seeking the well-being of the places its churches inhabit.

Church growth applies insights from the social and behavioral sciences to design methods of presenting the gospel that appeal to highly targeted audiences. Church growth models tend to emphasize methodologies, formulas and quantifiable results. Often associated with megachurches and seeker-sensitive churches, the church growth movement has been hugely influential, moving the goalposts even for many smaller churches that may not identify with church growth outright. Therefore, it's worth taking a little time to trace the outlines of the movement.

The father of the church growth movement is Donald McGavran, born in 1897, a third-generation Christian missionary to India. McGavran was a remarkable guy. He climbed the Himalayas, stopped a cholera epidemic and fought off wild animals. A graduate of Yale and Columbia, he was fluent in three languages.[7]

During the 1930s, McGavran was the executive secretary and treasurer for the United Christian Missionary Society in India. He oversaw eighty missionaries, as well as hospitals, schools and a leprosarium. It was during this period that McGavran noticed that, despite decades of hard work and hundreds of thousands of dollars spent, missionary efforts weren't yielding much fruit. He dedicated himself to "discarding theories of church growth which do not work, and learning and practicing productive patterns which actually disciple the peoples and increase the household of God."[8] (McGavran used the word *disciple* in the same way many of us would use the word *evangelize*. His word for the process of spiritual development—what many would call discipleship—was "perfecting.") He asked four questions: What are the causes of church growth? What are the barriers to church growth? What are the factors that lead to Christian movements? What principles of church growth are reproducible?[9]

McGavran never really stopped asking these questions, but in 1955, after leaving his desk job and planting churches for seventeen years, McGavran published a book about what he had learned so far: *The Bridges of God: A Study in the Strategy of Missions,* which has been called the magna carta of the church growth movement. Other books followed, including *How Churches Grow* (1959) and his classic *Understanding Church Growth* (1970). In 1961, Donald McGavran founded the Institute of Church Growth at Northwest Christian College in Eugene, Oregon. Four years later, he accepted an invitation from the president of Fuller Theological Seminary in Pasadena to open its third graduate school, the School of World Mission. Though he retired in 1981, he continued an active speaking and writing schedule until shortly before his death in 1990, at the age of ninety-two.

Gary McIntosh, a church growth advocate, has shown that the church growth movement has undergone several paradigm shifts over the last six decades. McGavran viewed church growth through the lens of a research paradigm, with a primary focus on international missions. But when church growth began to be used to address the needs of North American pastors, it took on first a business paradigm and then a marketing paradigm. Most recently, books like Rick Warren's *The Purpose Driven Church* and Stephen Macchia's *Becoming a Healthy Church* restated many church growth principles in the language of a church health paradigm.

CHURCH TECHNOCRACY

McGavran was especially interested in "people movements." In many cultures, he knew, the biggest decisions aren't made alone; they are made as families and tribes and as an entire community. He thus advocated using family and kinship ties as bridges to Christianize a whole people. He believed that people movements resulted in churches that were both quantitatively and qualitatively superior. "Instead of a conglomerate of converts from many different backgrounds who must learn to get along together," he said, "people-movement congregations are comprised of one kind of people accustomed to working and living together."[10]

But even though church growth has its roots in movement theory, it was soon promoting a kind of local church "technocracy," with an emphasis on strong top-down leadership, layers of management, more specialization, deeper reliance on marketing and the application of the scientific method, and as we will see, new kinds of compartmentalization. While we don't have space for a full critique, we do want to mention three troubling aspects of the modern church growth movement: its reliance on homogeneity, its static vision of church life and its focus on quantifiable results.

Homogeneity. Related to McGavran's people movement theory was his "homogeneous unit principle." He wrote: "People like to become Christians without crossing racial, linguistic, or class barriers. . . . The world's population is a mosaic, and each piece has a separate life of its own that seems strange and often unlovely to men and women of other pieces."[11] The church growth movement literature talks about "our kind of people" (the name of a book by C. Peter Wagner, McGavran's protegé) and says that, for the sake of the spread of the gospel, "segregation is a desired end."[12]

We see this segregation today not just in the racial and ethnic makeup of our churches, but also in the ways our church programs partition members based on age, gender, education level, hobbies, married or single, kids or no kids, working or retired. In contrast, the New Testament is clear that heterogeneity, *not* homogeneity, is the hallmark of the authentic kingdom. We are told in Colossians 3:10-11 that we have put on "the new self, which is being renewed in knowledge according to the image of its creator. In that renewal there is no longer Greek and Jew, circumcised and uncircumcised, barbarian, Scythian, slave and free; but Christ is all and in all."

Since slow churches seek to be deeply rooted in their individual neighborhoods, the tendency toward homogeneity might be inevitable. However, faith communities must constantly and proactively work against the inertia of uniformity. This is where the "rooted and linked" language of our friends over at the Parish Collective can be so helpful. The vision of the Parish Collective is to see churches, missional communities and faith-based organizations *rooted* in particular neighborhoods and *linked* to parish initiatives in other neighborhoods. When a small church from the suburbs comes together with an intentional community from the urban core, and a rural, faith-based arts organization commits to ongoing collaboration with a Spanish-speaking congregation comprised primarily of migrant workers, we get a glimpse of the reconciled diversity that is at the heart of the kingdom of God.

Of course, the demographics of neighborhoods change over time. When that happens, churches have the opportunity to reaffirm their commitment to their place and its people.

Mission stations. Early in his career, McGavran was a severe critic of the "mission station" approach to foreign missions. Mission stations were living relics of colonization. White missionaries moved into a new area and set up mission stations that often included hospitals, orphanages and schools. But they were usually separate from the local village and local culture; missionaries lived apart from the people they were trying to reach with the gospel. In addition, new converts were often pressured to Westernize, which McGavran believed slowed church growth because new Christians were separated from their families, and shoehorned into new ways of worship and dress and new ways of making cultural and ethical decisions. The time and energy missionaries devoted to running their social programs further slowed church growth. The mission station, McGavran wrote, "becomes an end in itself, instead of a means to the discipling of peoples."[13]

It's ironic, then, that churches that pattern themselves on church growth models tend to resemble the mission stations McGavran so disapproved of. They are Christian colonies, safe havens in an otherwise hostile and foreign world. They become ends in themselves, often devoting an enormous amount of time, energy and money to finding just the right "ministry mix"—new and bigger buildings, contemporary preaching, inspiring worship, abundant parking, excellent programs and a vibrant cell-group ministry—that will beef up attendance.[14] Members often feel tremendous pressure to conform to the mold of model Christian carefully prescribed by leadership and church culture. These churches almost always have a "come and see" mentality that limits church life to the four walls of a sanctuary rather than a mission that moves into the neighborhood.

Countable people. In *Understanding Church Growth,* McGavran makes the case that numerical growth is a key standard by which to judge the success of our efforts. "Jesus Christ, our Lord, came to seek and save the lost," he writes. "The lost are always persons. They always have countable bodies." He says later:

> The numerical approach is essential to understanding church growth. The church is made up of countable people and there is nothing particularly spiritual in not counting them.
>
> The numerical approach is used in all worthwhile human endeavor.[15]

However, one of the problems with church growth's emphasis on quantifiable results is that there is a strong temptation to be too pragmatic, ensuring that we "go and make disciples" not to the ends of the earth but only to those places where mission and ministry seem most likely to succeed. This is, in fact, one of the principles of church growth.

McGavran and Wagner use Jesus' parable of the lost sheep to bolster their case for the urgency of speedy and countable church growth. They say we spend too much time "peering into ravines where there are no sheep." But we think that parable is saying something very different, namely, that God often doesn't judge success by the same standards as "worthwhile human endeavors." Actually, Jesus told parables about a lost sheep, a lost coin and a lost son in Luke 15 because the religious elites of the day had been grumbling that Jesus was hanging out not with "our kind of people" (C. Peter Wagner's phrase), but with the "wrong kind of people," including tax collectors and sinners!

As Lesslie Newbigin and others have noted, the emphasis in Scripture is not on numbers but on faithfulness, as when Jesus says in Luke 18:8, "When the Son of Man comes, will he find faith on earth?"[16] The apostle Paul didn't seem to concern himself with the size of his churches. He didn't judge success by church growth. He was more concerned with following well in the footsteps of Jesus, and with his integrity as "a minister of Christ Jesus to the Gentiles in the priestly service of the gospel of God, so that the offering of the Gentiles may be acceptable, sanctified by the Holy Spirit" (Rom 15:16).

Bob DeWaay, the former pastor of Twin City Fellowship Church in Minneapolis, points out that by church growth standards, the greatest failures of all time were Noah and Jeremiah. Noah preached for a hundred years to no avail. Jeremiah's message was completely rejected. "Conversely, Jonah, if judged by Church Growth standards, was a fantastic success. The Bible does not see it that way." DeWaay also reminds us that the two churches that got the highest praise in the book of Revelation were Smyrna and Philadelphia, described respectively as being poor and having no influence (Rev 2:8-11; 3:7-13).[17]

Finally, it's worth noting that even by its own quantifiable standards church growth doesn't seem to be "working." According to Alan Hirsch, statistics from across the Western world "indicate that the vast majority of the church's growth comes from 'switchers'— people who move from one church to another based on the perception and experience of the programming. There is precious little conversion growth."[18]

THE McDONALDIZATION OF THE CHURCH

Church growth's reliance on "switchers" sounds distressingly like what happens when a big box store moves into an area. It doesn't create new shoppers; it just siphons customers away from the local mom-and-pop stores that can't possibly compete with the corporate giant's cheap prices and mind-boggling selection. I (John) live in Silverton, a small town known for its picturesque downtown, scenic surroundings and proximity to a beautiful state park. Silverton is growing quickly, but somehow it has managed to stay off the radar of many national restaurant and hotel chains. Before the 2010 census a rumor started going around town that if the new population totaled more than ten thousand, Silverton would automatically appear in a corporate algorithm somewhere and suddenly be overrun with Burger Kings and Holiday Inns. I can't verify whether the rumor was true, but I can confirm that many in the town breathed a sigh of relief when the population came in at ninety-nine hundred. Silverton's residents were concerned that the national chains would flatten our local flavor and culture.

In the introduction, we were introduced to George Ritzer's four key characteristics of McDonaldization. Efficiency, calculability, predictability and control have crept into many of our churches, flattening out the flavor of our witness before the watching world. Let's take a closer look at a few of the places we see these hallmarks of McDonaldization in the church, even in churches not necessarily associated with church growth.

Efficiency. In theory, to be efficient is to find the optimum means to a given end. However, quite often, whether in the workplace or the church, the word *efficient* is really a euphemism for *predetermined.* We see this in fast food joints, where employees are discouraged from finding new ways to do things, even if they might be more successful than the accepted methods. But it's just as evident in many books aimed at evangelical Christians—books that promise success, happiness, a deeper prayer life, intimacy with God, all in just "five easy steps."

Devotion to efficiency has a way of oversimplifying Christian discipleship. The "narrow way" Jesus talks about in Matthew 7 isn't a luge track we plunge into, in which every twist and turn is predetermined and our only job (not being Olympic athletes) is to hang on for dear life until the end, which is heaven. The narrow way is one we travel together without fear. The narrow way is fits and starts. It's running and walking and sometimes waiting. It's mountains and valleys and darkness and light. It's not being able to see the nose on our own faces and then things suddenly opening up into a magnificent vista. It's sometimes hard, but adventures usually are. It's not efficient; it's a conversation. You're more likely to go three miles an hour than seventy. You may feel alone but you're not. God is there. And look around you: a great cloud of witnesses.

Calculability. We've already seen how calculability—an emphasis on numerical results—has been used by proponents of church growth as a key way of measuring success. Calculability can make us slaves to speed and enemies of time. One-size-fits-all success models rarely allow time to discover the assets, needs, history, diversity, traditions and values of a community. (Mike Bowling, pastor of Englewood Christian Church, calls this "exegeting the place.") The models don't *take* the time because when you have confused quantity with quality, and when you believe you're racing the end of history, you don't *have* the time.

Slow Church operates from a perspective of time that is peculiar to our culture and peculiar even to the American church. We try to be purposeful but unhurried. Serving, as we do, a God who acts in time but is unbound by it, we can afford to enter a neighborhood with the posture of the listener. We can linger at the table. We can start work we won't see the end of. "Plant sequoias," urges Wendell Berry:

> Put your faith in the two inches of humus
> that will build under the trees
> every thousand years.

A Slow Church philosophy enables us to settle into the good, long labor of spiritual formation. Kyle Childress has been the pastor of

Austin Heights Baptist Church in Nacogdoches, Texas, for over twenty years. He tells us that there are some people who come into his church at eleven o'clock on Sunday morning looking for a deep spiritual experience but who want it instantaneously. They want a light show, exotic music and a dynamic speaker. But, Childress says, "there is so much about being a Christian that isn't like that. Slow Church is about taking the time with God, with one another, and with yourself—and not only taking the time, but taking time *over* time. That makes a big difference."

Predictability. Predictability is achieved when everyone and everything behaves in ways that are expected. "To achieve predictability," Ritzer writes, "a rationalized society emphasizes discipline, order, systematization, formalization, routine, consistency, and methodical operation."[19] There is something safe about knowing that the latte you order in a Boise Starbucks is going to taste the same as the one you drank in Spokane yesterday. It's comforting to know that the food, environment, prices and employee "scripts" will be the same from one McDonald's to the next. Predictability is what keeps people coming back to franchises. It's also what keeps people trying to franchise successful programs in the expectation of achieving predictable results.

John Drane, a professor of practical theology at the University of Aberdeen and the author of the spectacular book *The McDonaldization of the Church,* says that while Christians should try to learn from the success and failures of other churches, we shouldn't copy them. Our contexts are almost certainly too different. Instead, we should be asking ourselves what we need to do in our own unique circumstances. The people we recruit "to run ready-made programs are often the very ones who, with appropriate encouragement, might have had the energy and insight to create the experimental forms of worship and witness that could be transformational in their own local circumstances." He goes on: "It is easy to become so enamored with what God has done somewhere else that we fail to discern what God might actually do in this place and at this time."[20]

Control. Ritzer's fourth dimension of McDonaldization is the increased control of humans, often through nonhuman technology. We'll talk more about nonhuman technology in chapter six. For now it's enough to know that nonhuman technology includes not just machines but materials, skills, rules and regulations—anything that is used to control that greatest source of inefficiency, uncertainty and unpredictability: people.[21]

John Drane makes the important point that it is difficult to separate control from the first three categories of McDonaldization because control is the subtext of all the others.[22] We see control at work in the proliferation of satellite churches—separate, "branded" services that target specific populations through setting, style and ambiance while the sermon is piped in from the home campus. We see control at work in the church growth movement's emphasis on "visionary leaders" who are encouraged "not to be afraid of power."[23] C. Peter Wagner says that the pastor may appear to be a dictator but "to the people of the church his decisions are their decisions. They should realize that almost as if he had a sixth sense the pastor knows how to lead the church where the people want to go."[24]

Drane gives other examples of control at work in churches. He describes twentieth-century crusades where people who responded to altar calls were ushered through "an extensive process of spiritual socialization and control." He talks about cell-church strategies that are rigidly controlled from the top, never allowing cell groups to develop into fully functioning churches characterized by mutual support, encouragement and healing. Drane also mentions "lay ministries." The concept of lay ministries is deeply rooted in the New Testament. The problem comes when lay ministries aren't founded on

> any genuine commitment to the promotion of personal wholeness and the acceptance of God's kingdom. . . . It is

certainly striking that, for all our talk about releasing the gifts of the laity, most of our churches are only willing to release them to undertake the tasks that clergy would otherwise do, and if their innate gifts and talents are unconventional, we find it correspondingly difficult to change the system to create spaces for different things to happen.[25]

TASTE AND SEE

If McDonaldized church makes the case for increased efficiency, calculability, predictability and control, Slow Church makes "the case for taste"—specifically the case for "the taste of the place," and for "taste and see that the LORD is good" (Ps 34:8). Taste is the most intimate of the five senses. Seeing allows us to experience something from a great distance. Think of the vast expanse of land, water and sky—technically called a viewshed—visible to the human eye from the top of a high hill. Though our sense of hearing is not as far reaching as our sense of sight, we are still able to hear a crack of thunder or bells in a church steeple. Our range of smell is even closer. Touch closes the gap completely. We know that human touch is vital to physical, emotional and spiritual well-being, but it is still only surface to surface. Taste goes deeper. As Brother David Steindle-Rast, a Benedictine monk, has written, "Tasting what dissolves on our tongue dissolves the barriers between subject and object. What we have tasted we know 'inside out.'"[26] Thus to come to know the taste of a place is to blur the line between ourselves and the other. It thwarts the forces of alienation. As I become part of my place it becomes part of me.

Psalm 34:8 is an invitation to experiment. To taste God is to know God's goodness in the deepest way. When I (John) was young I was taught by someone that Jesus didn't actually expect us to do the things he said to do in the Sermon on the Mount. Instead, Jesus was setting the bar impossibly high so that we could know beyond a shadow of a doubt that we couldn't rely on the law anymore. We would have no option but to fall back on his grace. But I know better now. Jesus clearly intended us to do the things he said to do. In fact, he says so twice in the Sermon on the Mount (Mt 5:19; 7:24-27)! He says in John 14 that anyone who loves him will obey his teachings. Elsewhere he says that the "disciple is not above the teacher, but everyone who is fully qualified will be like the teacher" (Lk 6:40).

We find out who Jesus is along the way. We walk the way with Jesus, only to discover that Jesus himself has been the Way and also the destination. Jesus invited people who were skeptical about his teachings to try them on for size: "Anyone who resolves to do the will of God will know whether the teaching is from God or whether I am speaking on my own" (Jn 7:17). This is the language of experimentation and a call to apprenticeship.

THE GOSPEL OF THE COFFEE BEAN

Tasting God's goodness and costly discipleship go hand in hand. As we follow Jesus, we experience in new ways the complex palate of God's goodness. Similarly, since the church is the body of Christ, it is partly through the church that the world tastes God. This is why Slow Church refuses to sacrifice quality to quantity. When efficiency, calculability, predictability and control become the primary standards by which we evaluate our life in our churches, it's easy to justify cookie-cutter approaches to disciple making. Churches churn out Christians notable not for their authentic peculiarity but for their bland sameness. The final standard needs to be faithfulness.

There is a connection between tasting and seeing that the Lord is good and the *saltiness* of the church. Jesus says in Matthew 5:13 that we are "the salt of the earth." Jesus' salt metaphor is a potent one for a first-century culture that used salt as a preservative, to season its sacrifices, to help fire its earthen ovens and to flavor its food. Salt is a vital resource, and yet it is a humble one. It draws out the inherent flavor of a food while still remaining uniquely itself. Salt has a tendency to dissolve, and there is something of Christlikeness in that. We're reminded of Paul's exhortation to the Philippians to

> do nothing from selfish ambition or conceit, but in humility regard others as better than yourselves. Let each of you look not to your own interests, but to the interests of others. Let the same mind be in you that was also in Christ Jesus,
>
> > who, though he was in the form of God,
> > did not regard equality with God
> > as something to be exploited,
> > but emptied himself. (Phil 2:3-7)

As coffee lovers, we sometimes think of the gospel as a coffee bean. We can't experience the pleasures of coffee directly from the bean. It is experienced indirectly, as the bean is roasted (put through the fire, so to speak), ground to a powder and subjected to boiling water. We're confident that God desires for us to find joy and deep pleasure in our local faith communities, but we're equally convinced that it is futile to seek that joy directly. One of the great paradoxes of the gospel is that we find supreme joy indirectly as we go through the fire, are ground up and poured out for each other. This process of giving ourselves up for one another is at the very heart of the way of Jesus, "who for the sake of the joy set before him endured the cross, disregarding its shame, and has taken his seat at the right hand of the throne of God" (Heb 12:2).

The very elements of the Eucharist—the bread and the wine, the symbols of Christ's being poured out on our behalf—imply the grinding and baking of the wheat and the stomping and patient fermenting of the grapes. In our consumer culture, we are constantly being bombarded with messages that urge us to seek happiness, usually by pulling out our wallet. But Jesus said something very different—that "those who want to save their life will lose it, and those who lose their life for my sake will find it" (Mt 16:25). It is in the context of the local *ekklesia* that we learn how to be poured out for one another and for our neighbors.

CONVERSATION STARTERS

1. What things—for instance, people, practices, convictions— define your congregation and give it its distinctive taste? How can we celebrate these things in a way that does not vainly "puff up" but rather bears witness to the transforming work of God?

2. What things bring the greatest joy to your congregation? Which celebrations are most anticipated each year? Why are these celebrations met with great joy, and how did they come to be so?

3

Stability

Fidelity to People and Place

. . . Hope
Then to belong to your place by your own knowledge
Of what it is that no other place is, and by
Your caring for it as you care for no other place.

Wendell Berry, from "Sabbath Poems 2007, VI"

I (Chris) have on the shelf by my writing desk a lovely little nature book called *The Apple Tree Community*, first published in 1960. The author, George Smith, describes in stories, short vignettes and photos the diverse community of creatures that gathered around an ancient apple tree on his farm. Smith begins the book with the story of a woodsman who dropped by his farm one day with an axe and offered to chop down the tree. "You can burn the pieces (of the tree) in your fireplace," the woodsman said, "and you can plant a new, young straight one in its place." Smith politely declined the man's offer, saying that there was much more to the tree than met the woodsman's eye. "That old apple tree is a honey factory, a bird's hotel, a summer cafeteria, a winter pantry, a concert stage, an egg hatchery, a nursery, a shelter, a floral exhibit. It's even more," he went on; "it's the center of a patch of green earth where daisies, buttercups, goldenrod and evening primroses grow."[1]

The tree was able to bear fruit and offer hospitality to the "apple tree community" because it was rooted in place and had matured in that place over many decades. Similarly, in order to bear fruit, to extend hospitality and to nurture a flourishing community, our faith communities must be deeply rooted and maturing in *our* particular places. The good and abundant life God intends for creation is nurtured through the interdependency of God's creatures, and this interdependency—as the apple tree community reminds us— flourishes best when we stay put over a long period of time.

HOW GOD'S MISSION OF RECONCILIATION UNFOLDS

Let's pause for a moment to consider the great diversity of God's creation. Limiting our focus to Earth—just one of an estimated 100 billion planets in the Milky Way, which is itself just one of *at least* 175 billion galaxies in the universe—and limiting ourselves even further to dry land, think of the brilliant variety of landscapes, climates, peoples, languages and cultures. Think of the natural diversity in your own backyard. Oregon, where John lives, is roughly the size of Ecuador, but it is a state of extremes, featuring a rugged coastline, dramatic river gorges, pluvial lakes, snow-capped mountain peaks, fertile valleys, lush, temperate rain forests, and high desert. The diversity of creation is evident at even the smallest levels. A single teaspoonful of healthy garden soil can contain thousands of species, millions of organisms and up to a hundred meters of fungal networks. Healthy soil is so abundantly manifold that only about 1 percent of soil microorganism species have even been identified.

The mission of God in the world is centered on the redeeming and reconciling of a diverse creation. How does God intend to accomplish this reconciliation? One of the great flaws of McDonaldization is its preference for generic, one-size-fits-all solutions. A restaurant chain is more efficient, more predictable and easier to control, and its successes and failures will be easier to quantify, if every restaurant is identical in its architecture and operations. But the more we consider the wonderful diversity of God's creation, the more skeptical we must become about the possibility of universal solutions. God is reconciling all creation, but this reconciliation unfolds in a manner that is attentive to, not dismissive of, diversity. Specifically, it is embodied by faith communities of all stripes whose members are being reconciled to God, to one another and to their neighbors.

Jesus, for example, was born in a manger in Bethlehem, among a particular people at a particular time in history. He gathered around himself a community of twelve disciples, a number that recalled the twelve tribes of Israel. Ezekiel's vision of the dry bones coming together, taking on sinew and flesh and finally breath (Ezek 37:1-14), came to fruition in the life and work of Jesus; Israel was being resurrected as a people.

After Jesus' death and resurrection, his disciples dispersed throughout the world and planted churches that were manifestations of Christ's body in their particular places. These early church communities shared life together in such a way that they were maturing together into "the full stature of Christ" (Eph 4:13). Australian theologian Robert Banks has observed in his superb book *Paul's Idea of Community* that "each one of the various local churches [in Paul's day] is an expression of the heavenly church, a manifestation of that which is essentially eternal and infinite."[2] The church has historically spoken of Christ's coming to earth as his incarnation—his enfleshment. Christ's incarnation isn't limited to the first century. It continues into the present through the church—the body of Christ—through communities of believers who are faithfully rooted in their places, embodying Christ in ways that can be experienced and known by the particular people who live in those places.

Slow Church puts this continuous incarnation of Christ's body at the heart of God's plan for reconciliation. God is redeeming creation place by place by gathering communities of people who, like the ancient apple tree, mature, flourish and lovingly engage their neighbors. But in order for the good, joyous and freeing reign of God to leaven creation, there must be a commitment to rootedness, a virtue the Benedictines have long called *stability*.

In many monastic traditions, monks and nuns take a vow of stability, committing to remain all their lives in their local communities. The Rule of Benedict says, "The workshop where we are to toil at all these tasks [of Christlikeness] is the enclosure of the monastery and stability in the community." The vow of stability from Our Lady of the Mississippi Abbey, a Cistercian monastery in Dubuque, Iowa, reads as follows:

> We vow to remain all our life with our local community. We live together, pray together, work together, relax together. We give up the temptation to move from place to place in search of an ideal situation. Ultimately there is no escape from oneself, and the idea that things would be better someplace else is usually an illusion. And when interpersonal conflicts arise, we have a great incentive to work things out and restore peace. This means learning the practices of love: acknowledging one's own offensive behavior, giving up one's preferences, forgiving.

It is difficult for us to bear witness together to the patient and delectable way of Jesus when people are cycling rapidly into and out of our churches. Few of us are called to be monks or nuns. And yet, there is a lot we can learn from the monastic tradition about sharing life together in a community of God's people. Stability is one virtue that is essential to our incarnational understanding of God's mission.

HYPERMOBILITY AND INDIVIDUALISM
The greatest challenges to stability in churches today are hyper-

mobility and individualism. Hypermobility has become a fixture of contemporary Western culture. More and more, we experience the world from inside our cars, whether we're crawling in rush-hour traffic or zipping down the interstate at seventy miles per hour. Americans spend nearly three hours a day in their cars. The number of people who commute to work in private automobiles increased from 41 million in 1960 to 120 million in 2009, and traffic congestion now costs the average commuter thirty-four hours a year in the form of delays and hundreds of dollars in wasted gas. Many of our cities and suburbs are so built to accommodate the automobile that cyclists and pedestrians can feel disoriented, even at-risk, in their own neighborhoods.[3]

I (Chris) didn't realize how deeply I had been formed by hypermobility until I sat down a few years ago to write a review of Jonathan Wilson-Hartgrove's book *The Wisdom of Stability*. By that time I'd been a member of Englewood Christian Church for over five years; as I wrote my review, I began to reflect on my own experience. I realized that in the decade prior to coming to Englewood, I had lived at twelve different addresses in four different states. Raised within the ethos of individualism, I had spent that decade following the educational and career opportunities that seemed best for me—college, summer internships, a full-time job in a global corporation, grad school, an internship with a church, and then back into the corporate world. My life was ordered according to the narrative of self. The price I paid for chasing that story, despite the many friends I made along the way, was my isolation from a particular place and a community of people. I moved around so much that I belonged to no place. I tell my story here not because it's unique but because it's so common. By some estimates, Americans now change residences an average of fourteen times in their lives.

In Western culture, we are also profoundly shaped by the ethics of individualism. We learn early on to follow our own stories wherever they may lead us. We hear a lot these days about capital-S Story, about the power of story, about crafting more exciting and more meaningful life stories, and so on. The metaphor of *story* is a resonant one, but there are some pitfalls to be aware of too. The first potential pitfall is that we can judge ourselves too harshly when things don't go as planned. There is so much we can't anticipate about the arc of our lives that we necessarily spend a lot of time and energy responding to fate rather than mastering it, being shaped by life rather than shaping it. Instead, we need to learn to hold loosely to our scripts because we're not the sole authors of our stories.

The second pitfall is that by chasing the stories of self we become tourists of life. There is a great scene in season two of the television show *Parks and Recreation* that makes just this point. Ron Swanson, the director of a small town parks and recreation department, is explaining to his assistant director, Leslie, why she doesn't like her boyfriend, a guy who is by all appearances a decent and successful man. "He's a tourist," Ron says. "He vacations in people's lives, takes pictures, puts them in his scrapbook, and moves on. All he's interested in are stories. Basically, Leslie, he's selfish. And you're not. That's why you don't like him."

The vital question is: what is the primary story around which we shape our lives? Careening from one thrilling story to the next like an adrenaline junkie, we may be successful, we may even be doing good in the world, but we will also leave a lot of broken relationships in our wake. The down times, the slow work of spiritual formation, the dailyness of apprenticing ourselves to Jesus, the long-term commitment to particular people and a particular place—all the quotidian details of life will leave us restless and discontented. If, however, we find our identity primarily in the scriptural story, we begin to understand community and place as integral to God's reconciliation of creation through the continuous incarnation of Christ in the world.

DISPLACED, DISEMBODIED CHRISTIANITY

Duke Divinity School professor Willie James Jennings, in his recent book *The Christian Imagination,* has powerfully described the damage wreaked on Western culture by disembodied religion, including damage to human relations and to creation at large. "I want Christians to recognize," he says, "the grotesque nature of a social performance of Christianity that imagines Christian identity floating above land, landscapes, animals, place and space."[4] Disembodied Christianity abandons the realities of place and all but ensures that our interactions with creation will be dictated by narratives like materialism, capitalism and individualism that are rooted in something other than Scripture. This arrangement is ripe for propagating a host of social and ecological injustices. Consider colonialism. The horrific effects are plain to see in the lives of the native peoples who were killed, displaced, enslaved and subjugated. But there is also tragedy in the displacement of the colonialists who didn't value their roots in Europe and were compelled—often by narratives of greed—to move.

In the twentieth century, disembodied faith combined with the rise of the automobile to drastically alter the experience of Western Christianity. Our friend Brandon Rhodes, the "Grassroots Storyteller" of the Parish Collective, has been researching the effects of the automobile on culture, and particularly on American Christianity. "From drive-in churches and church reader boards to seeker-sensitive, market-savvy and multisite megachurches, many evangelical churches have adapted to suburbia phenomenally," he says. "That is, they provided the religious goods and services for a car-shaped America better than anyone else."

The increase in mobility led to a shift in the organizing principle of churches. For centuries, proximity was paramount. People went to the church that was closest to their home—or they attended the church that met in their home! But with the rise of the automobile, choice became primary. With the elevation of choice, it didn't take long for churches to be defined by their homogeneity. Rhodes quotes Gibson Winter's 1962 book, *The Suburban Captivity of the Churches*:

> Congregations are explicitly organized around similarity in social and economic rank; in fact, their survival generally depends upon the degree to which they can maintain likeness in their memberships. A few highbrows and a few low-brows can be thrown into the congregational mix, but the core has to be drawn from similar occupation, income group, educational level, ethnic background, and residential level if the congregation is to survive.

If we remember what Donald McGavran and C. Peter Wagner said about the "homogenous unit principle," we're reminded that a well-meaning monoculture is at the heart of much of the church growth movement, which helped further dis-place and dis-embody Western Christianity.

The church has experienced the same kind of "clustering"—a reorganization toward homogeneity—as other segments of community life, including the economy, politics, voluntary associations and the fabric of neighborhoods.[5] Advances in technology and infrastructure, combined with an ethos of transience, make it all too easy to just find a new church when conflicts arise—as they inevitably will—rather than staying and working them out. (The familiar description of this process as "church shopping" hints at how closely it is tied to individualism and materialism.) When we give preeminence to our own stories over the story of God's work in the church, we lose first the *motivation* and then the *capacity* to work through difficult situations.

As we grow deeper in our church communities and more fully rooted in our places, it's important that we create spaces where we can talk openly. Rather than running from conflict, or battering the opposing side until it surrenders, we need to learn (or relearn) how to work through problems together. Fifteen years ago, Englewood Christian Church set aside Sunday nights as a time for open discussion, and that conversation continues today. Initially, there were four or five "factions" within the congregation, each with their own distinct theological perspective. The first few years were extraordinarily volatile, and a few people left. But those who stayed put and in conversation found, over time, that while the conversation didn't always lead to an agreement, it did help build trust, particularly with those with whom they disagreed.

THE MOBILITY OF CHURCHES

In addition to the transience of their members, churches themselves face a crisis of hypermobility. Many churches have put down only shallow roots in their neighborhood, or no roots at all. We've all heard the question, "If our church suddenly moved to a new location fifteen miles away, would anyone in our neighborhood notice we were gone?" But what if we asked ourselves this question: "If our church was magically lifted off the ground and moved to a location fifteen miles away, would *we* notice the difference?" Western churches have become so disentangled from their own places that this question could be a cold, hard look in the mirror for many faith communities.

Many of our churches *are* moving, if not by magic. In Indianapolis, Lincoln, Los Angeles, Shreveport, Falls Church and Salem, in towns and cities across the country, churches are migrating away from the city center. They are lured to greener suburban pastures by the prospects of cheaper land, ambitious building projects and abundant parking. When contemplating church flight, we need to ask ourselves another question: "What kind of witness do we bear to the neighbors we leave behind?"

One of the great legacies of the Roman Catholic tradition is the notion of the parish: churches that are rooted in particular places, among the people that live there. Protestant churches could learn a lot from Catholic parishes like St. Philip Neri in my (Chris's) Indianapolis neighborhood, which recently celebrated one hundred years of being a church in the same location. St. Philip's history is notable because they have persisted in the same location despite many challenges, including severe persecution from the Ku Klux Klan in their early years and a drastic shift in the demographics of their congregation over the last quarter century (from mostly white to mostly Spanish-speaking). Unless churches today can recover a sense of parish responsibility, of belonging to people and place, we will continue to propagate the disembodied Christianity—and its accompanying racial, social and ecological injustices—that Willie Jennings described.

What if our church grows too large for our present facilities? One answer is that instead of moving to newer and larger facilities—a transition that will come with a hefty price tag—consider planting new churches that can be rooted in different places. Instead of sending a single church planter or a small handful of people, why not bless a community of people, those who live in or near a different neighborhood than the existing church, to start their own church? This was the vision that helped the church spread like wildfire during its first few centuries of existence. There should be a healthy conversation between the sending church and the planted church, but each should be free to take the shape that is appropriate for its neighborhood. As families often do for their adult children, the mother church provides counsel and some resources, but the planted churches are free to grow and mature in their vocation.

I (Chris) grew up in a congregation within the Grace Brethren fellowship of churches that began as this sort of church plant. The mother church was in a suburb of Washington, D.C., but by the late 1970s it had essentially maxed out the capacity of its facilities. Given its prominent location, it couldn't acquire any adjacent property for expansion. So, instead of uprooting the congregation and moving to a place where land was plentiful and cheap, the church found members on the perimeters who lived in close proximity to each other and who were willing to start their own local church plant. At least four congregations were started in this way, forming almost a full circle with the mother church at the center. My parents were among the group that started the southernmost of these new congregations. The connection between the church plants and the mother church was very loose; each congregation took shape according to the place they inhabited and according to the gifts and skills inherent among the people God had gathered there.

My (John's) parents go to Salem Alliance, a large Christian and Missionary Alliance church in downtown Salem, which is about twenty-five minutes from my town of Silverton. Not long ago, Salem Alliance had the opportunity to buy a choice piece of land on the outskirts of town. Moving there would have made it easier, in terms of parking and larger facilities, to accommodate its growing congregation. But Salem Alliance made a bold decision. They decided not to move the church but instead to reaffirm their commitment to their struggling Grant/Highland neighborhood. They used money from the building fund to buy a piece of property across the street from the church, and they built what is now called Broadway Commons, a gorgeous forty-seven-thousand-square-foot space that includes clinics that offer free medical and dental care to the uninsured and underinsured; meeting rooms open to the community; the Broadway Life Center, which provides quality yet inexpensive educational and vocational opportunities for families in the neighborhood; professional office space; an outdoor plaza with a waterfall and an amphitheater; a prayer center called The Upper Room; and Broadway Coffeehouse, the best coffee shop in the whole city, a place where the craftsmanship of coffee is taken seriously, though never at the expense of hospitality. True to its name, Broadway Commons is a place where very different kinds of people come together. In the words of John Stumbo, the former pastor of Salem Alliance, Broadway Commons was to be "a place where church, commerce and community come together for the common good."

CULTIVATING KNOWLEDGE OF A PLACE

This brings us to another crucial question, one of the most pressing for churches in the early years of the twenty-first century: How do we begin to cultivate stability, as individuals and churches? Maybe the place we're in is not the sort of place that we would have chosen to be. Maybe we don't like the place we are. One way to tackle these challenges is to get to know our neighborhoods in intimate ways. "To feel at home in a place you have to have some prospect of staying there," says the wise Kentucky farmer-poet Wendell Berry. He writes elsewhere: "[Hope] to belong to your place by your own knowledge / Of what it is that no other place is."[6] Place, like all things in life, is a good gift from God. Our calling is to come to know our places in ways that reveal God's gifts to us and that evoke in us deep gratitude and rejoicing—which is to say, worship.

One of the books that has been most formative for me (Chris) is Parker Palmer's *To Know as We Are Known,* which advocates teaching and learning in a way that nurtures deep knowledge. In the book's first chapter, Palmer describes this kind of knowledge: "[Our minds] were given to us for another purpose: to raise to awareness the communal reality of nature, to overcome separateness and alienation by a knowing that is loving, to reach out with intelligence to acknowledge and renew the bonds of life."[7] We will return to the "the communal reality of nature" in chapter five, but for now let's consider the question of how we come to know our place in such a way that we grow over time to embrace it.

To achieve a "knowing that is loving" we need to learn the rhythms of the person, place or thing we are seeking to love. Rhythm is essential to learning. This is true of learning music, obviously, but also of learning physical activities and language. (Punctuation is a type of rhythm; consider the important difference between the rhythms of "Let's eat, Grandpa" and "Let's eat Grandpa.") Rhythms are learned through attentiveness over time. This becomes harder, especially with regard to our places, when we move around so frequently and when we don't make an effort to connect with those folks who have lived in our neighborhoods for many years and who carry the wisdom and memories of the place. To know the rhythm of a place is to know, for instance, what summers and winters are like and to have experienced enough seasons that we recognize when the weather takes a peculiar, unseasonal turn. To know a place is to know when the daffodils bloom, when the birds fly south for the winter and when to expect the first frost. Places have natural rhythms. They also have civic, economic and social rhythms reflected in elections, taxes, sales, festivals, local holidays and school calendars. These rhythms help define a place. The challenge of our time is to learn and engage with the rhythms of our places.

This is a challenge that's been driven home for me (Chris) over the last decade. Englewood has many of the characteristics people expect of an inner-city neighborhood: crime, a large homeless population, pothole-ridden streets and high levels of transience among our neighbors. If I could have picked an ideal place to live, this would *not* have been it. Englewood is a dull-looking, gritty place, the landscape is flatter than a sheet of plywood, and on the surface of things it looks like a rather dead place. The power of stability, though, is the chance to get below the surface, to recognize patterns, to become more sensitive to the work God is doing all around us.

In the years I have called Englewood home, I have come to deeply love this place. The neighborhood has changed a little, but not all that much; instead, I am the one who has been most changed. Three things stand out as particularly transformative in my process of coming to know and love Englewood. Above all, I am a member of a church that is deeply involved in the neighborhood and values the neighborhood—despite its outward appearances—as a good gift from God. Our church community is active in getting to know our neighbors, spending time with them both working and relaxing together. The church and its neighbors are engaged in the intense work of helping our neighborhood flourish.

A second factor was my role in helping spearhead a local history project. In collaboration with the Englewood Neighborhood Association, which brings neighbors together to collaborate for the good of our place, we worked to chronicle the story of our neighborhood. The deeper I got into the research, the more amazed I was at the familiar all-American names who had visited our neighborhood or who had been affected by work that went on here: George Washington Carver, Elvis Presley and Barack Obama, to name just a few. Though Englewood is tiny, it plays a role in some huge American stories. (I suspect that most places have similar sorts of links to familiar stories if we would only uncover them.) One example is the rundown house the church is fixing up right now. This house was once the home of Reb Russell, a big-league ballplayer who was teammates with Shoeless Joe Jackson and friends with Babe Ruth. Legend has it that Russell and Ruth would sit on the front porch of this house and drink together until the early hours of the morning. As the stories were uncovered in our project, they gave meaning to this place, and meaning to my place in it, both as an individual and as a member of a church whose history is nearly as old and storied as the rest of the neighborhood.

Another important factor in my coming to love Englewood is my adventures in urban naturalism. Cultivating stability in our congregations requires practices that help us be attentive to all facets of human and natural life in our neighborhoods. Inspired by the poetry of agrarian writer Liberty Hyde Bailey, I explore my neighborhood, tuning my eyes and ears to all the gifts that God has given in the plants, animals, rhythms and landscape of this place. These adventures include a mix of walking, exploring, bird watching, tree climbing and learning. Several years ago, my kids and their friends discovered an ancient catalpa tree in the yard next to ours whose trunk had been hollowed out by the forces of nature to such an extent that two small children could fit inside. This tree was an amazing gift that our kids spent hours playing in and on. In the same yard is a large mulberry tree, which during the early weeks of summer produces purple berries that are messy and prone to stain but that also make a mighty tasty jam.

There is good work for churches to do in helping their members deepen their knowledge of their neighborhoods. This work could easily dovetail with Christian education programs that are already in motion. One of my most memorable experiences in urban naturalism was the several months I spent with a group of homeschoolers from our church studying Pleasant Run, a little creek that is our nearest natural water source. At its closest point, Pleasant Run comes about four blocks from the southeast corner of our neighborhood. We used Google Maps to trace the length of the creek from its source to its mouth, where it empties into the White River on the city's south side. We discussed how you could, if you were a mouse with a very small boat, float from just outside our neighborhood all the way down to the Gulf of Mexico. We drove and walked almost the full length of the creek, watching for animals that drew life from the stream, measuring the speed of its current. We talked about why the stream was polluted and often smelled of raw sewage and about ways we could reduce the pollution.

We need practices that will reorient our desires to our places. Such practices will vary widely across the diverse spectrums of individuals, churches and places, but the story of Chris's transformation is a reminder that change is possible. What if our churches took the lead in organizing neighborhood storytelling projects? What if they collected oral histories of the neighborhood and found innovative ways of archiving and presenting them? In fact, why not combine oral history with the opportunity to tutor/mentor neighborhood kids who are interested in filmmaking? The kids can interview community residents old and new (teaching them interviewing skills), collect old photographs and maps and relevant physical documents, and then write a script (teaching them English language arts). Then they can work with a mentor to create mini-documentaries about a local resident or an aspect of local history. These films can be premiered at a film festival in your neighborhood—perhaps even in the church. This is just one idea, but it reminds us that it is possible to reorient our desires toward the places we live, but it requires intentionality. We find it helpful to think of this reorientation as a kind of spiritual discipline. As with all spiritual disciplines, the most important part isn't the techniques we employ but the end itself.

God is transforming creation. If we slow down and stay put long enough, we too will be changed into the likeness of Christ. The scope of our vision will also be changed. Instead of speaking in broad generalities about changing the world, we will find ourselves free to imagine in more specific ways the transformation of our own particular places. We can trust that God is orchestrating the renewal of all creation and that God will raise up people in other places who will care for those places as much as we care for ours.

CATALYZING LOCAL CULTURE

The rich and abundant life of God flows outward from our church communities and helps our neighborhoods become places that matter and, ultimately, places that flourish. Churches become catalysts of local culture. In his helpful book *Culture Making,* Andy Crouch describes this work as an act of cultivation. Just as the farmer works the land to cultivate his crops, so we work with the good gifts God has given us in our places. We come to know these gifts intimately and work them together to continue the cycle of cultivation. Crouch says:

> Cultivating natural things requires long and practiced familiarity with plants and their place; cultivating cultural things requires careful attention to the history of our culture and to the current threats and opportunities that surround it. Cultivation is conservation—ensuring that the world we

leave behind, whether natural or cultural, contains at least as many possibilities and at least as much excellence as the one we inherited.[8]

Cultivation of our communities involves attentiveness not only to the rhythms of our specific places but also to the day-to-day sorts of choices we make and the sort of rhythmic order we impose on those places. As our roots grow deeper in a place, we can't help but want to see that place thrive. Seeking the flourishing of our places involves not only caring for them—keeping them clean, planting gardens, living lightly on the land—but also caring for the people who live here with us, of course. One significant way of caring is the practice of regularly buying food and other things we need from locally owned and locally sourced businesses. This economic activity is a way of loving and caring for our neighbors. Local farmers and artisans return the care by providing foods and goods that are healthy, well made and durable.

Other sorts of artists—musicians and visual artists, for example—help us to understand and interpret our landscape, language, history and culture. I (John) started a local arts cooperative in Silverton called the Upstream Makers Collective. Upstream is a community of visual and performing artists, designers, writers and storytellers, musicians, farmers, gardeners, craftspeople and makers of all kinds who are committed to collaboratively developing their cultural gifts and using them for the flourishing of people and the land. We describe our work as fostering rural culture for the common good. But the scope of that work is hyper-local. We find it creatively and socially invigorating to confine our vision to the Molalla-Pudding River "cultureshed," which includes the towns of Silverton, Mt. Angel, Stayton and the unincorporated lands in between.[9]

The Upstream Makers Collective promotes public art installations, leads a creative-asset mapping initiative, facilitates community storytelling, hosts book clubs, and supports the work of local culture makers, among many other things. In 2014, we're holding our first annual FRED Talks, which will feature TED-style talks and curated conversations on the art of neighboring. (The conference is named FRED as a hat-tip to Mister Rogers.) Another new project is designed to serve faith communities in our area through arts and culture. We're encouraging churches to display visual art in their lobbies, sanctuaries and other public spaces. And we're trying to support them as they integrate art and storytelling into the life of their communities while nurturing their own home-grown makers. Supporting artists and nurturing the gifts of artists in our congregations, we help tell the stories of our communities and cultivate our places in ways that are distinctively local.

HOSPITALITY AND GENEROSITY

It's important that our stability is characterized by hospitality and generosity, two economic practices of Slow Church that will be addressed in more detail later in the book. Two of the gravest dangers that often accompany stability are (1) seeing ourselves as superior to those who are new to our place, especially those whose transience is not of their own choosing, and (2) using our embeddedness to accumulate wealth and power. This is the difference between rootedness and entrenchment. Christian hospitality compels us to welcome all strangers, regardless of how they found their way to our door or how long they plan to stay. Similarly, developing habits of generosity—sharing the resources God has given us—reminds us that stability is not a means to attain status. Stability is always oriented toward the health and flourishing of our places. It is never an end in itself.

We have been called to nurture culture and life. The people God gathers in a place are uniquely gifted to embody the freeing and healing good news of Jesus together. We embody Christ by loving God and loving one another—forgiving and restoring each other when we fail to act in Christlike love. Romans 12 offers us a vivid image of the cultivating work of the church. Though we have a diversity of gifts, "we, who are many, are one body in Christ" (v. 5). Verses 9 through 18 give shape and direction to our life together:

> Let love be genuine; hate what is evil, hold fast to what is good; love one another with mutual affection; outdo one another in showing honor. Do not lag in zeal, be ardent in spirit, serve the Lord. Rejoice in hope, be patient in suffering, persevere in prayer. Contribute to the needs of the saints; extend hospitality to strangers.
>
> Bless those who persecute you; bless and do not curse them. Rejoice with those who rejoice, weep with those who weep. Live in harmony with one another; do not be haughty, but associate with the lowly; do not claim to be wiser than you are. Do not repay anyone evil for evil, but take thought for what is noble in the sight of all. If it is possible, so far as it depends on you, live peaceably with all.

Our churches can be the means through which God's healing love is poured out on our particular places today. Our joy, our hope, our patience, our generosity, our hospitality, our humility, our peaceableness—these virtues, which essentially mirror Paul's fruits of the Spirit in Galatians 5, are the gifts of God cultivated over time, like the apples on an apple tree. It is not difficult to see in today's over-sexualized world, a deep but often misplaced longing to love and be loved, or, in drug abuse or consumerism, a misplaced longing for joy. As we abide in Christ together (see Jn 15:5-8), we bear good fruit that feeds a hungry world.

The fruit we bear will be most succulent when we stay rooted in a place and in a community of other Jesus-followers. There are times for sending people from one church to another—a grafting of branches, to continue the horticultural metaphor. Such sendings, however, should be the exception and not the rule, and they should be the result of discernment and blessed as part of the work of the church, rather than viewed as accidental in the course of an individual's pursuit of his or her own fulfillment. If our churches are indeed manifestations of Christ's body, and if we as individuals are to abide in Christ, we must stay rooted in a church community. We can no longer afford to propagate the modern, Western illusion that communities and places are irrelevant. In fact, they are built into the very fabric of God's diverse creation and are essential to its reconciliation.

CONVERSATION STARTERS

1. What is the story of your congregation? Have you always existed in your current location? If not, where were you located before, why did you move and what were the effects of your move on the church and the former neighborhood? If you have always been in your current location, have there been times when the congregation was tempted to move, and what factors led to resisting that temptation?

2. Pick a radius appropriate for your context (shorter for urban places, longer for rural). Identify all the churches within that radius. How have you gotten to know those congregations and to work together with them? If there have been no such opportunities to date, how can you move in the direction of collaboration?

3. How many people leave your congregation in a given year? Is there any recognition of their leaving? What conversational practices do you have (or could you develop) for helping people discern whether they should stay in or leave your congregation?

4. Where are the third places—neither home nor work—where people gather in your neighborhood? Are there members of your congregation regularly engaged in those places? How can they build stronger bridges between your church and the neighborhood? If not, who in your congregation might be encouraged to become engaged in that third place?

4

Patience

Entering into the Suffering of Others

[Patience] fortifies faith; is the pilot of peace;
assists charity; establishes humility; waits long for repentance;
sets her seal on confession; rules the flesh; preserves the spirit; bridles
the tongue; restrains the hand; tramples temptations under foot;
drives away scandals; . . . consoles the poor; teaches the rich
moderation; overstrains not the weak; exhausts
not the strong; is the delight of the believer.

Tertullian, *Of Patience*

Our homes are many-altared temples to the gospel of instant gratification. In the kitchen, the microwave gets our food piping hot in
minutes. The refrigerator keeps food fresh and ever ready for prep-
aration and consumption. The dishwasher cleans a mountain of
dirty dishes with minimal labor. Hot water is available throughout
the house on demand. Machines wash and dry our clothes.
Flushable toilets immediately dispose of our bodily waste; no more
going out to the outhouse in the dead of winter or having to empty
the smelly contents of chamber pots.

If we crave entertainment, we turn on the television, where we have access to literally hundreds of channels. We can play games on the Wii. And thanks to Netflix streaming, we have a huge library of shows and movies for every member of the family available at any time of day or night. Through our smartphones and wireless laptops, we can find the news and information we want on the Internet. Google measures down to the fraction of a second how fast it can search the entire store of recorded human knowledge. If there is something we want to buy—say, a book or crafting supplies—we order them with just a few clicks of the mouse, and they arrive on our doorsteps in a matter of days.

The built environment—our homes, workplaces, church buildings and shopping malls, and the roads that connect them all—serves to both reflect and feed our desire for convenience, which in turn is fueled by impatience. In their profound book *Compassion: A Reflection on the Christian Life,* Henri Nouwen, Donald McNeill and Douglas Morrison define impatience as an "inner restlessness . . . [that is,] experiencing the moment as empty, useless, meaningless. It is wanting to escape from the here and now as soon as possible."[1] If we as God's people have any hope at all of slowing down and savoring the richness of life and God's abundant goodness, then we have to address this impatience that lies deep in our hearts.

Patience, as Nouwen, McNeill and Morrison explain, can be understood as a third way between the polar extremes of fight and flight. In patience, we learn to abide in each particular moment, finding it not empty but rather full of the grace of God. How do we grow deeper into our calling as the patient people of God when our surroundings reinforce our inner restlessness? That is the question at the heart of this chapter.

THE EMERGENCE OF A CULTURE OF IMPATIENCE

Western culture, and increasingly global culture, is built on impatience. The inner restlessness of humanity is nothing new, but for at least two centuries, the quickening march of technology and

industrialization has formed us into a culture of instant gratification—which is another way of saying instant dissatisfaction.

The Industrial Revolution that emerged in Great Britain in the
second half of the eighteenth century was an era in which the means
of producing goods began to shift from manual labor and the power
of draft animals and the home to machine-powered factories. The
textile industry was one of the first to be radically transformed. Prior
to the Industrial Revolution, textile making involved gathering fiber
from sheep or cotton plants, preparing it and spinning it into threads
that could be woven or knitted into cloth. This lengthy, intensive
process was usually done in the home, by local craftspeople. In fact,
this is the origin of the phrase "cottage industry."

The invention of the flying shuttle in 1733 dramatically sped up
the weaving process, and it was one of the most significant steps in
the mechanization of the industry. With the emergence of coal-
powered steam engines, and technologies like the Spinning Jenny
(1764), textile making was soon fully mechanized. Other industries
followed suit, including agriculture and metallurgy. Industrialized
transportation—steam boats, railroads and the automobile—soon
made the transport of goods easier, faster and cheaper.

Mechanization was good at making stuff faster, and it was good
at making a few people very wealthy. But it also escalated pollution,
produced starvation wages and led to worker abuse. It's no accident
that the enduring image of the Industrial Revolution is William
Blake's "dark satanic mills."

The Industrial Revolution gave birth to the cult of speed celebrated in the Futurist Manifesto, a devotion that would eventually
go mainstream in a culture of impatience. The culture of impatience
didn't create human restlessness; it fed it. It *served* this dangerous
aspect of human nature so that eventually it could be *served by*
human nature. It's not a stretch to think of impatience as a biblical
power or principality.

Of course, the effects of human restlessness have rippled

throughout creation. The costs of technological expedience can be seen clearly in our insatiable appetite for energy—from the gasoline that powers our cars to the coal that is burned in order to generate electricity (after whole mountains have been leveled to get at it), to the use of nuclear power and all the hazards and wastes and thousand-year half-lives that come with it. Every time we use our car or a power tool, we are contributing to pollution. Our demand for energy contributes to catastrophes like the nuclear meltdown at Three Mile Island or the BP oil spill in the Gulf of Mexico. We aren't suggesting that it's possible to stop using coal or petroleum power. But we should carefully consider the sometimes hidden costs of our impatience and the sacrifices of convenience we might be called to make as followers of Jesus.

OUR AVERSION TO SUFFERING

Our devotion to speed, and our reliance on labor-saving devices and techniques (more on this in chapter six), raise pressing questions:

- To what end are we saving labor?

- What kind of space are we creating in our lives by eliminating labor? What will we do with that space?

- By reducing or eliminating labor, are we creating space for sloth and idleness, sabotaging our attentiveness to details and undermining the opportunities for good work done well?

As we will see in later chapters, people were created to work. One of the key tensions created by technology is the tension between the goodness of work and the crushing consequences of overwork or, in theological terms, between the goodness and necessity of work and our call as the people of God into a sabbath life. Nicholas Wolterstorff speaks powerfully of the tension between technology and its boundaries in his book *Lament for a Son,* his theological meditation on the death of his twenty-five-year-old son in a climbing accident:

We live in a time and place where, over and over, when confronted with something unpleasant we pursue not coping but overcoming. Often we succeed. Most of humanity has not enjoyed and does not enjoy such luxury. Death shatters our illusion that we can make do without coping. When we have overcome absence with phone calls, winglessness with airplanes, summer heat with air-conditioning—when we have overcome all these and much more besides, then there will abide two things with which we must cope: the evil in our hearts and death. There are those who vainly think that some technology will even enable us to overcome the former. Everyone knows that there is no technology for overcoming death. Death is left for God's overcoming.[2]

To borrow language from Wolterstorff, Western culture, in all its technological grandeur, has become obsessed with overcoming suffering. Certainly, there are some sorts of suffering that should be overcome if we are able, but our call is to compassion—a word derived from the Latin meaning "to suffer with." The great tragedy of our technological success is not just that we've created a culture that avoids suffering, but that we have lost the capacity or willingness to enter into the pain of others. "Although I'm sure it has never been easy to be present with and to those who are suffering," says theologian Phil Kenneson, "our culture's three cardinal virtues [productivity, efficiency and speed] powerfully disincline us to placing ourselves among those who weep. Few people seem genuinely willing to slow down and offer real presence to those who otherwise weep alone. As a result, so many among us suffer in deadly silence and isolation, devoid of any real human contact, let alone real presence."[3]

Our avoidance of suffering dilutes our witness to our Lord Jesus, who took our suffering upon himself in love. When we can't enter into the sufferings of our sisters, brothers and neighbors, the Christ

we embody in our neighborhoods is a shallow distortion of the
Jesus we encounter in Scripture. The rich flavors of gospel that we
are called to convey are watered down. The avoidance of suffering
leads us to take shortcuts that steer us clear of human pain, difficult
situations and hurt people. Neighbors who struggle with mental
illness or homelessness need people who will walk with them as
friends and bear some of their burdens. But this intimate calling
demands much of us. Too often our faith communities prefer to
outsource deep care by giving people in need food, clothing or
money and then sending them on their way.

Patience is how compassion is embodied in our lives. Nouwen,
McNeill and Morrison have observed that "patience is the hard but
fruitful discipline of the disciple of the compassionate God." They
go on to challenge the notion of patience as passive waiting, noting
that this false conception is often used by those in power to keep
marginalized people under control. "[Not] a few among those in
very influential positions have counseled patience simply to avoid
necessary changes in church and society. . . . [Rather,] patience
means to enter actively into the thick of life and to fully bear the
suffering within and around us."[4]

Defining patience this way reveals the error not only in avoiding
the suffering of others but also in trying to fix their suffering of
others without entering into it. The road toward healing and reconciliation is the patient, compassionate way of Jesus.

PATIENCE AMONG THE EARLY CHRISTIANS

As we seek to mature in the patience and compassion of Christ, we
should look to the example of the first Christians.

Patience was a formative value for the early churches, and church
fathers like Origen and Tertullian wrote detailed treatises on the
subject. The early Christians had something more in mind when
they used the Latin word *patientia* than how we think of patience
in the early twenty-first century. For them, patience was what we

might call longsuffering. The *patientia* they saw embodied in the
life, death and resurrection of Jesus taught them that it was better
to suffer than to inflict harm. The tight-knit social dynamics of
the early churches made it possible—and even necessary!—to
embody the *patientia* of Jesus in ways foreign to those of us who
live under the influence of Western individualism. The early
Christians believed that, in a very real way, God had created a new
family, a community of brothers and sisters under one Father,
who journey together on the difficult way of discipleship and who
carry each other's burdens when they become too much for us to
bear on our own.

Tertullian's third-century meditation on *patientia* vividly describes its significance to community life. He begins by emphasizing God's patience:

> [God] scatters his blessing of light equally over the just and
> the unjust; he allows the benefits of the seasons, the services
> of the sun and rain and snow, indeed all the blessings of
> nature, to fall upon the worthy and the unworthy; he bears
> with the most ungrateful nations, worshipping as they do the
> toys of the arts and the works of their own hands, persecuting
> his Name together with his family; he bears with luxury, greed,
> iniquity, and all sorts of evil, waxing insolent daily.

In regard to human patience, Tertullian says *patientia* denies our
cravings for revenge. It is also closely connected to the virtue of
love. He reminds us that the first word used to describe love in
1 Corinthians 13 is *patience*. As an example, Tertullian points to
Jesus' teaching that we should forgive a person who sins against
us not just seven times, but seventy times seven.

Tertullian advocates bodily patience as well as spiritual patience.
By bodily patience, he meant denying the lusts of the flesh through
simplicity of diet and drink, fasting, the church "accustoming
herself to sackcloth and ashes." By disciplining our bodies, he

argues, we will be prepared when our bodies are subjected to persecution, including prison and martyrdom—very real threats in that time and place. Our English word *martyr* comes from the Greek meaning "witness." Christians who have died for their faith bear witness to the resurrection through which Christ conquered death. Christians in the Western world face little or no persecution. But learning from the bodily patience of the early Christians can help us bear witness to the gospel of Christ Jesus.

Fasting and other forms of self-discipline are important not primarily because they make us better individuals but because they remind us that the Story that gives us our identity is not primarily about me and my desires. If we practice simplicity, for example, we will have more resources to share with others and can bear witness to God's generosity. If we strive to be healthy, we will be better prepared to give ourselves in expressions of care for others—working diligently in witness to Christ's gospel of compassion.

Tertullian concludes by telling the biblical stories of those who patiently bore in spirit and body the temptations and persecutions that assailed them. These include Stephen, Isaiah and especially Job:

> For by all his pains [Job] was not drawn away from his reverence for God; but he has been set up as an example and testimony to us, for the thorough accomplishment of patience in flesh as well as in spirit, in body as well as in mind; in order that we succumb neither to damages of our worldly goods, nor to losses of those who are dearest, nor even to bodily afflictions.[5]

The stories of the martyrs were widely circulated among the early churches. Through the persecution and suffering of its members, the first Christian communities were energized to offer a poignant alternative to the often brutal pagan ways of the Roman Empire. Modern churches must begin to rediscover a longsuffering that can be a testimony of the empathic love of Jesus.

LEARNING PATIENCE IN THE LOCAL CHURCH

The local church is the crucible in which we are forged as the patient people of God. We have been united with each other in the life, death, resurrection and ascension of Jesus. As we mature together into the fullness of Christ (Eph 4:13), over time and in our places, we learn patience by forgiving and being reconciled to one another. Our brothers and sisters may incessantly annoy us. But we are called in Christ to love and to be reconciled to them. Just as marriage vows serve as a covenant bond that holds a couple together in difficult times, our commitment to our faith community is essential if we are to learn patience and practice stability. Patience can hold us together when other forces conspire to rip us asunder.

The forces of fragmentation often emerge through the sufferings of others—including financial difficulties; addiction to pornography; infidelity; the alienation of members based on economics, race, age, sexual orientation and so on; and fears that lead to divisive behaviors like gossip and power grabbing. In those difficult times, it's natural for us to want to fix these struggles from a distance or to run from them altogether. But we learn patience by immersion, journeying faithfully alongside those who are suffering. It's easy, for example, to lob advice or judgment when a friend's marriage is falling apart. It's more complex, and more demanding, to sit down with the couple, to listen, to work slowly and conversationally toward healing, to celebrate reconciliation or to grieve a divorce.

Some members of our churches will inevitably leave, be sent elsewhere or die, but our commitment to grow deeper with the same people in the same place—come what may—will provide a rich context through which God will bring forth fruits of the Spirit (Gal 5). The health and fruitfulness of a plant diminishes each time it is uprooted. In the same way, our growth toward patience is stunted each time we uproot ourselves from the sustaining soil of our local community. As we learn patience through the exercise of compassion in the local congregation, it flows outward from our church, making us more patient with neighbors, coworkers, other churches, community groups, civic officials and people with whom we do business.

In the decade since I (Chris) have been a part of the Englewood Christian Church community, my sisters and brothers here have taught me much about compassion. There was one five-year period during which my wife and I were especially worn down. We were raising three very young children, one of whom was adopted as a toddler. We grieved the loss of a stillborn daughter. Our preschool-age son was diagnosed with cancer. And we were shocked by the unexpected death of my wife's father. Through all this, the church community was there, providing us with flexible work, helping financially at several points along the way, and taking care of all the funeral arrangements (and costs) for our daughter Hazel. But most important of all, they were just *with* us. They didn't feel the need to bombard us with religious platitudes. Grief, as Wolterstorff and others have observed, is isolating. Our family experienced that isolation, but we also had a deep, reassuring sense that our brothers and sisters were entering into that suffering with us.

In a recent lecture he gave on Slow Church, theologian Phil Kenneson told the story of something that happened at the United Methodist church he belongs to in eastern Tennessee. On Christmas Eve 1989, as the church was preparing to celebrate, they discovered that the ten-story building across the street was on fire. This building was the largest in the city, and it served as apartments for the low income and elderly. The church immediately canceled its holiday service. It became an operations hub for firefighters and rescue personnel, a triage center, and even a morgue, as sixteen people lost their lives. Kenneson observes:

Needless to say, it was a sobering Christmas Eve. But one long-term effect on the congregation was to make it more attentive to its downtown neighbors. Sometimes the beauty of the world grabs your attention; at other times, tragedy does. Many members confessed to having previously paid scant attention to the folks who lived right across the street from our place of gathering. . . . And so the church began to examine ways it might be a better neighbor to these long-neglected folks across the street. So by the time [conversations] arose about moving to the suburbs [almost a decade later], the church was for the first time becoming involved with its neighbors. And this was the reason the congregation decided to stay, to abide, in downtown Johnson City. We believed we were there for a reason and that to leave would involve not merely abandoning an address and piece of property, but would mean abandoning these neighbors with whom we were trying to be in relationship. And so we stayed.[6]

The Eucharist is one important way we are reminded of our call to enter into the compassionate life of Jesus. This sacrament, consisting of real food and drink, highlights the connection between the ecology of God's reconciliation of all things (discussed further in chapter five) and God's transformation of our desires so that we become a more patient and diligent people.

William Cavanaugh has observed in his superb little book *Being Consumed: Economics and Christian Desire* that although we take the bread and the cup of the Eucharist into our bodies, it is we who are being consumed by it. We are absorbed into the interconnected life of God's creation. Just as Christ becomes food for us, we give ourselves away and become food for others. We see that there is no room for us to be mere consumers—people who take without giving—and that "things" (including technology, programs and all the accoutrements of a McDonaldized society) must be evaluated in light of how they bind us together with God and humanity.

> We are not to cling to our things, but to use them for the sake of the common good. . . . We must understand where our things come from and how our things are produced. Things do not have personalities and lives of their own, but they are embedded in relationships of production and distribution that bring us into contact, for better or for worse, with other people's lives. . . . At the same time, a sacramental view sees things only as signs whose meaning is only completely fulfilled if they promote the good of communion with God and with other people.[7]

Our desires are transformed as we submit ourselves to the eucharistic life of Christ. Additionally, as Cavanaugh says above, the most important factor we should consider in making the choices that give shape to our lives is not "Will it cause pain and suffering?" but rather "Will it move us in the direction of the common good?"

CONNECTING OUR ENDS WITH OUR MEANS

From Machiavelli to innumerable military operations to "make the world safe for democracy," we are enthralled by the idea that the ends justify the means. But the subversive way of Jesus teaches us the opposite: that living by the sword means dying by the sword and that the means will determine the ends, not the other way around.

That means the good ends for which we are striving can't be separated from our means. The "ecology" of Slow Church is embedded in the interconnectedness of creation and God's reconciliation of all things. This is the theme of the next part of the book, but it is directly relevant to our call as the church to compassionately enter the suffering of others.

For almost a decade, Englewood Christian Church ran a food,

clothing and furniture pantry in its neighborhood. Driven by a desire to love our neighbors, we handed out thousands of dollars of goods every week. But after years of doing this, we found that it had had little transformative effect on our neighborhood. Friendships weren't being forged. Lives weren't being radically changed. In some instances, we were probably even doing harm by fostering dependency on our handouts. So we decided to wind down the pantry ministries and find new, more engaged ways of caring for our neighbors. Rather than handing people stuff and sending them away, we tried to meet personally with people who came to the church with needs. We became immersed in comprehensive community development that partners with our neighbors to make the Englewood neighborhood a better place to live. What sparked this change was that we became increasingly attentive not just to our end (caring for our neighbors) but to the means by which we could best reflect the love and peace of Jesus.

In a familiar passage in John 14, Jesus describes himself as "the way, the truth and the life." Eugene Peterson writes in *The Jesus Way*:

> [The] means? In a word, Jesus. Jesus, pure and simple. If we want to participate (and not just go off in a corner and do our own Jesus thing), participate in the end, the salvation, the kingdom of God, we must do it in the way that is appropriate to that end. We follow Jesus. . . . We cannot pick and choose ways and means that are to our liking.[8]

Our tendency as Western churches is to shift, out of impatience, to the logic of "by any means necessary." Picking up our crosses and following Jesus is messy and painful and slow, so we justify any action with the hope that it will lead to the kingdom of God. Jonathan Bonk's wonderful book *Missions and Money*, for instance, chronicles the disastrous results of foreign missionaries who can't or don't live on a similar economic scale as their neighbors, which often leads to the propagation of pseudo-colonialism. Many churches are oblivious to this kind of collateral damage: Jesus is being proclaimed; why should it matter how missionaries live?

THE PATIENT PEOPLE OF GOD

We can't escape the question of what might it mean to say that Jesus is the Way.

First, it implies that our churches are the embodiment of Christ and essential to God's work in the world. Churches, including intentional communities, house churches, local congregations and larger associations of congregations, are the primary way in which Christ's followers are to work in the world. Eugene Peterson says, "A Christian congregation, the church in your neighborhood, has always been the primary location for getting this *way* and *truth* and *life* of Jesus believed and embodied."[9]

Monastic communities have long taken seriously the challenge to daily embody the way of Jesus in their particular places. In sharing life together as a community, and not simply being a weekly gathering place for individual Christians, every facet of life—home, work, worship and so on—requires discernment about whether it conforms to the reconciling way of Christ. Though tradition, context and local adaptation all ensure that the rhythms of our churches will look much different, traditional churches have much to learn from monastic communities about embodying Jesus together in a place.

Second, to follow Jesus challenges us to be attentive to God's reconciliation of all creation. Action rooted in hatred, greed or partisanship of any sort is not in step with the Jesus Way. We need spaces in our church communities where we can discuss and discern together in this direction. We need the manifold wisdom of God embodied in the whole of our church communities to make decisions that are attentive to God's love for and reconciliation of the whole creation.

Many multiethnic churches are seeking to bear witness to Christ's reconciliation of all humanity. Living Water Community Church in the Rogers Park neighborhood of Chicago, for instance, follows a vocation of participating "in Christ's work of reconciliation in our church, neighborhood and world," and is a diverse congregation with services in Khmer (Cambodian), Nepalese and English, as well as a Swahili choir. Reflecting the diverse ethnicities of their urban neighborhood, the congregation is learning to bear witness to our unity in Christ by regularly eating and celebrating together and by discerning together. Other churches bear witness to Christ's reconciliation in different ways. Six central Indiana congregations recently collaborated to secure a grant to install solar panels on their buildings. Most non-Amish churches use electricity, and many are becoming more attentive to how much electricity they use, but these Indiana congregations bear witness that we are not constrained to use destructive sources of electric power forever. These examples hardly do justice to Christ's reconciliation of all things, but their stories are poignant reminders that we need to be continually seeking to grow in the vast, reconciling love of Jesus.

Finally, to follow Jesus as the Way means that we must take all his teaching seriously, even the difficult ones like "Turn the other [cheek]" (Mt 5:39), "Love your enemies" (Mt 5:44), and "Whoever has two cloaks must share with anyone who has none" (Lk 3:11). We know we are on shaky ground when we start rationalizing *why* we don't have to follow Jesus' teaching, rather than trying to put them into practice in our church communities and neighborhoods. In order to discern the way of Jesus, we need to have a deep knowledge of who Jesus is and what he taught. Although we are called to actively bear witness to Christ's reconciliation, we also need to be continually studying the biblical texts together in our local churches, seeking to know Jesus better in order that we might embody him more faithfully in our particular place.

If our churches hope to mature into healthy and robust em-bodiments of Christ, then we must constantly be seeking to follow Christ together compassionately in our everyday life—our means of Christlikeness must fit our ends. Our many failures to be attentive to our means seem hypocritical to outsiders, and even many insiders. We claim to follow Jesus and generally do have a deep desire for the kingdom of God, but the means by which we bear witness to God's reconciling work look very little like the way Jesus showed us to live. A slow church is one that seeks to follow in the Way of Jesus day by day, even when doing so seems inconvenient or even impossible. A key part of our slowing down as churches is taking the life and teachings of Jesus seriously, not ignoring them or rationalizing them away but really seeking to embody Jesus together within all the particularities of our own neighborhoods.

Confession, then, is a mark of Slow Church. We have to face the truth about ourselves. We confess that we have conformed to the impatience of Western culture. We acknowledge the social and ecological costs of this impatience. And we submit ourselves to God's transformation in our local church communities. Our congregations are embodiments of Christ in our particular places. It is there we must learn to follow in the way of the man of sorrows—a way that was, in compassion, well acquainted with patience of body and spirit, with grief, and eventually with torture and death.

As communities of people who are rooted and maturing in our attentiveness to the patient and reconciling way of Jesus, the pace of our life together will inevitably slow down. Our attentiveness together will mold us into a people that bears witness to the rich goodness of the gospel of Jesus. As we cultivate practices of stability and patience, growing deeper into our calling as local communities of God's people, we become increasingly aware of God's work of restoration—not just among God's people, but throughout all humanity and all creation. We explore this ecology of reconciliation in the next part of the book.

CONVERSATION STARTERS

1. If Jesus is not only the person that we are to embody together in our neighborhood but also the Way in which we are to do so, then who do we understand Jesus to be? What did he teach? How did he live? And how are these questions related?

2. Reflect on times when you have acted impatiently as a congregation. What was driving your impatience? What were the outcomes of your impatient action? What would you do differently if you were faced with a similar situation now?

3. In what ways do you as a church enter into the sufferings of others in your church or neighborhood? Tell stories of times when you have failed to enter into (or to enter fully into) the sufferings of others.

Second Course

ECOLOGY

5

Wholeness

The Reconciliation of All Things

*[Can] I separate my own health from
the rest of the world? My own good nutrition from the
poor nutrition of billions? My longing for peace from the warring in
the Middle East . . . or anywhere else at all? In a universe where the
lifting of the wings of a butterfly is felt across galaxies, I cannot
isolate myself, because my separation may add to the
starvation and the anger and the violence.*

Madeleine L'Engle, *A Stone for a Pillow*

One of my (Chris's) favorite movies is Darren Aronofsky's psychological thriller *PI*. The film centers around a bizarre character
named Max Cohen. Max lives an isolated life, barely talking to the
other characters in the movie, and he is obsessed with numbers.
He believes everything can be reduced to numbers, and he uses his
prodigious math skills to make stock market predictions. Eventually, he stumbles upon a 216-digit number that keeps popping
up repeatedly. Launched into a surreal sequence of events, he is
driven deeper and deeper into madness. The movie ends with Max
giving himself a homemade lobotomy by punching a power drill
through his temple.

PI vividly depicts how the isolation and reductionism of our times—Max's compulsion to reduce everything to numbers and equations—can ultimately lead to madness. Max's tale is even a kind of disaster film. Madeleine L'Engle keenly observes in her book *A Stone for a Pillow* that our English word "disaster" comes from the roots *dis-* (meaning "separation") and *-aster* (meaning "star"). Disaster is thus a separation from the stars, a fragmenting of creation, the shattering of what God formed as an interconnected whole.

It's a distressing sign of our times that the dark and outlandish story of *PI* has a ring of truth to it. Western culture has been shaped under the ever-tightening grip of technology and individualism, and the trend of modernity has been toward greater isolation from people and places. At the same time, we have been trained well to compartmentalize our lives and narrow our vision. Like Max Cohen, we reduce life to broad generalities. We approach people not as unique persons created by God but as generic categories: African American, Latino, female, gay, wealthy, homeless, liberal, right wing and so on. We use these labels most often with people who are different than us. It's natural for us to communicate using shorthand, but relying too much on categories can put up walls between *us* and *them*. It denies people their individuality, while focusing overly much on how we are different from each other rather than what we have in common. Reductionism is therefore a rebellion against the fundamental unity of God's diverse creation.

FRAGMENTING AN INTERCONNECTED CREATION

The fragmentation of our lives is disaster and alienation and madness, and we are only beginning, in the last fifty years, to see the cultural cracking and crumbling that are the fruit of the ideologies of individualism, consumerism and fast life. Although it's presumptuous to say that these cultural conditions cause mental illness, it is widely recognized that they exacerbate it. They also have a highly destructive effect on the health of the planet as a whole. It's well known, for example, that the United States comprises 5 percent of the world's population but consumes 30 percent of the world's resources. According to the Sierra Club's Dave Tilford, the average American, in his or her pursuit of "the good life," consumes as many resources as thirty-five people from India and fifty-three people from China.[1]

Is this fragmentation built into the structure of creation? We emphatically answer *no*! God who is triune—three distinct persons and yet a united whole—created many distinct forms, living and nonliving, that are united in an interconnected whole we call creation. We're learning more about this interconnectedness in recent decades, in the work of mathematicians and physicists and ecologists. One of the most elegant examples is the butterfly effect. In 1961, an American mathematician and meteorologist named Edward Lorenz was working on a computer model for weather predictions. He was attempting to repeat one weather pattern. But instead of entering the six-digit number .506127 into his computer, he entered the three-digit .506 to save time. He expected the same weather pattern to appear. But what appeared, Nancy Mathis has written, was radically different. "He'd assumed that the difference of one part in ten thousand would be minimal, that the picture that emerged would be at least similar to what he'd seen before. Instead, the two patterns bore no resemblance to each other."[2] Lorenz went on to write a landmark research paper on chaos theory, in which he described the way seemingly insignificant actions can lead to huge consequences. he also offered a new iconic metaphor to help people visualize his theories: he asked, Can a butterfly flapping its wings in Brazil set off a tornado in Texas?

Although we can articulate the three-in-one nature of God, the exact ways in which the three sovereign persons interact and are connected are largely a mystery to us. Similarly, we have a radically incomplete understanding of how creation is woven together as a singular whole. We can describe discrete relationships in the vast web of creation—for instance, dietary relations (this animal eats these plants) and geographic relations (these creatures live in proximity to one another)—but we've only scratched the surface of, and will never fully grasp, how a nearly infinite number of created forms are united in the network of creation.

Not only is creation an interdependent whole, all of creation has already been reconciled in the death, burial, resurrection and ascension of Christ. Even now, God is at work orchestrating the fulfillment of this reconciliation. "In [Christ,]" the apostle Paul says, "all things in heaven and on earth were created, things visible and invisible . . . all things have been created through him and for him. . . . And through him God was pleased to reconcile to himself all things, whether on earth or in heaven, by making peace through the blood of the cross" (Col 1:16, 20).

In his recent book *Salvation Means Creation Healed: The Ecology of Sin and Grace,* theologian Howard Snyder examines the dynamics of God's reconciliation to a broken creation. Snyder employs the language of ecology:

> In an ecological understanding, everything is related to everything else. The study of ecosystems helps us grasp the nature of these interrelationships and learn how to work for stable and flourishing systems, overcoming the maladies that harm or even destroy an ecosystem over time. . . . [This] ecological conception is biblical at heart and can be an important tool in helping us understand the comprehensive healing message of the gospel.[3]

As the people of God, we locate ourselves in the ecological story of God reconciling an interconnected creation. But it's extraordinarily easy for us to lose sight of this narrative and to narrow our focus. Industrialization's modus operandi is to pick a particular problem—say, producing a faster and cheaper widget—and hone in on finding solutions to this problem with little or no regard for the costs or effects that might be borne by the broader creation.

Consider some of industrialism's "solutions" that have opened a Pandora's box of new problems:

- Industrialized agriculture provides access to cheap food, but it comes at the cost of denuded land, the loss of topsoil, animals raised in brutal conditions, toxic fertilizers and pesticides, the loss of traditional farm knowledge, a staggering amount of debt accrued by farmers who were told to "get big or get out," bankruptcies, rural population flight, and the rise of multinational seed companies that wield an enormous amount of power over what is grown and eaten in this country.

- The automobile opens up new horizons for autonomous travel, but it comes with unintended consequences like pollution, environmental hazards, rapid climate change and the devastation of many small towns as well as urban neighborhoods that suddenly empty of people who can afford to commute to work from the suburbs.

- The rise of plastics addressed many important concerns about hygiene and distribution, but they increased our reliance on petroleum. They are also virtually indestructible. We have no good way to dispose of them since they will not decompose.

- We appreciate being able to buy affordable clothing. But these clothes are often made in sweatshops in Southeast Asia, sometimes by children.

These economic shortcuts have often led to the degradation of human life and culture, as well as wide-scale environmental destruction: shrinking polar icecaps, water shortages, toxification of soil, extinction of species, and on and on. During the writing of this chapter, we read an interesting statistic from Greenpeace. The earth is believed to be 4.6 billion years old. If we scaled that to 46 years, humans have been on the planet for about four hours. Since the dawn of the Industrial Revolution one minute ago, we have destroyed half the world's forests.

If Christians acknowledge these catastrophes at all, there is a temptation to view them as irrelevant to our faith and practice. "It's all going to burn anyway," we've heard more than one Christian say. Here again we see the fragmentation of life and thought. Our lives are cleft into the spiritual and the material. Into home and work and church life. Into the global North and the global South. Even the life and work of our churches has been deeply shaped by the fragmented thinking that fails to consider the whole of creation and God's pursuit of its reconciliation.

Focusing too narrowly on one thing, our "personal" relationship with Jesus, for example, we become inattentive to the consequences our actions might cause outside the area of our focus. Irish philosopher and theologian Peter Rollins sees this shortsightedness as the crux of a crisis facing Western churches in the early twenty-first century. He poses these pointed questions:

> What if the love you affirm and the fruits of the Spirit you seek to share in your daily life actually mask a deeper illness that encourages the very opposite of these fruits at a structural level? What if the problem is not one of certain parts being corrupt, but rather of these parts being symptoms of a much deeper and more far-reaching corruption?[4]

In the Sermon on the Mount, Jesus says, "The eye is the lamp of the body. So, if your eye is healthy, your whole body will be full of light; but if your eye is unhealthy, your whole body will be full of darkness. If then the light in you is darkness, how great is the darkness" (Mt 6:22-23). The word *unhealthy* in this passage can also be translated "stingy." Being inattentive to the living web of God's creation—for example, not recognizing that the twelve-year-old girl sewing my shirt in Bangladesh is just as much my neighbor as the family next door—is to have stingy eyes. God wants us to go through life with eyes wide open. Not only will we walk more gently on the earth, we'll be more available to experience the wonder of a God who stoops low to feed the birds and clothe the lilies (Mt 6:25-34).

DUALISM

Let's consider a few examples of the fragmentation of our lives and survey the damage it wreaks in our churches. Perhaps the oldest and most prominent of these fractures is the dualism of matter and spirit (or body and soul). Although few people would state it so baldly, elevating the spiritual over the material leads to the mindset that it doesn't matter what we do to Earth because our home is in heaven and God is going to destroy and remake the world anyway.

A 2010 study by the Pew Research Center found that religion has far less influence on opinions about environmental policy than other factors. Just 6 percent of respondents said their religious beliefs were the biggest influence, compared to the 26 percent who cited the media and the 29 percent who cited their education. Similarly, a study conducted by researchers from Purdue University in the late 1990s found that evangelical Christians had higher rates of obesity than the American population at large. The obesity rate was even higher among Christians devoted to a literalist reading of Scripture. Those who took biblical "condemnations of the flesh" (Rom 8:1-13; Gal 5:16-24) literally were seemingly inclined to be less careful about the stewardship of their own bodies.

Although it doesn't have particularly deep theological roots (and in many ways reflects the individualism of the larger culture), the Daniel Plan for weight loss, developed by Rick Warren at Saddleback Church, is an important step in the right direction. It recognizes that our bodies matter. Furthermore, Saddleback's experience—the congregation shed over 250,000 pounds in its first year on the Daniel Plan—is a hopeful sign that congregations can work together toward a shared life that is more holistic and healthy. Warren attributes Saddleback's success in this endeavor largely to the solidarity, encouragement and accountability that participants found in their small home groups. Warren notes: "What we discovered is that people who signed up for The Daniel Plan who were in a small group lost twice as much as those who did it on their own."[5]

We slip into dualism when we make a false distinction between our faith and the rest of our lives. We participate in church services on Sundays, but we don't allow our faith to shape the rest of our lives—our choice of jobs, for example, or how we do the necessary work these jobs demand. Most Christians desire to do good work that fits with their faith, but through fragmentation, they find they are largely on their own as they choose a career path, find a job and carry out their daily work.

In my (Chris's) experience, I got some advice from my parents, as well as some basic biblical principles of right and wrong from my parents and our church, but I was pretty much free to pick a career and prepare for it. I was never encouraged to consider my vocation within the scope of our particular church and place. Rather, I was left to navigate in the dim light of abstracts: seeking a good job that didn't offend Christian principles and that paid a handsome sum of money (an abstract measure of economic activity). Once I landed a full-time job, I never considered how that work fit within the life of my church. My story reflects the fragmentation of our culture. Even now that I am seeking a vocation within a particular church community and place, it is still difficult to set aside the individualistic forms of decision making that were drilled into me for the first thirty years of my life. In retrospect, I see that I was left to make major decisions apart from my *people* and my *place*. I lacked a community that could help me discern a vocation. And I learned that the most important thing was my *career*—a word that abstracts work from the rest of life—not the place in which I pursued good work.

We all compartmentalize our lives. If our work isn't at odds with our faith, then perhaps our play is. How often do we scrutinize our entertainment in light of Christ's reconciliation of all things? Are we, in Neil Postman's famous words, amusing ourselves to death? Does our entertainment isolate us from others, as is the tendency with many personal electronic devices (mp3 players, smartphones, handheld video gaming devices, etc.)? And what are the social and ecological costs of our entertainment—for example, the cost of electricity or gasoline we use to pursue frivolity or the costs of the mineral coltan, the mining of which is being used to fund the conflict in Congo?

Obviously entertainment is not all bad, but we have to be open to scrutinizing every corner of life. If Christ is reconciling all creation, then we walk on dangerous ground when we wall off certain areas of our life, shielding them from the transforming light of Christ, who said "I am the light of the world. Whoever follows me will never walk in darkness but will have the light of life" (Jn 8:12).

NATIONALISM

Nationalism fragments our lives by causing us to privilege one nation above another. For centuries, God-and-country theology has helped justify death and destruction at an almost unprecedented level. Nazi Germany and the recent wars in the Middle East are just a couple recent examples. American exceptionalism gave us Manifest Destiny and the theology-soaked atrocities committed against Native Americans, and it's still alive and well today.

When we're under the aegis of nationalism, we forget that God is reconciling all creation, and it becomes too easy to demonize other nations and inflict all manner of destruction upon them. Thus, we have Christians from the United States killing Christians from Europe in the First and Second World Wars (and vice versa, of course) and, as Emmanuel Katongole has noted in his book *Mirror to the Church,* Hutu Christians slaughtering Tutsi Christians in Rwanda, one of the most deeply Christian countries in Africa. The conviction that, in Christ, God has reconciled all humanity and all creation leaves no room for nationalism.

With a quick glance at the World section of today's newspaper, one is confronted by stories of conflict in Mali and Syria, mounting tension in Israel/Palestine and the Korean peninsula, car bombs in Baghdad and Kano and Mogadishu, and the ongoing US war in Afghanistan. As one conservative radio host used to say, war is about killing people and breaking things. It can be difficult to imagine how Christ's reconciliation will be brought to completion in the midst of so much bloodshed and destruction. But this is the context of the slow *missio Dei* into which we have been called. Nationalistic faith is a shortcut around trusting God to carry out God's mission of reconciliation. Nationalism is also a shortcut around our call to be peacemakers.

Not only is God reconciling all humanity, but the church is central to that reconciling mission. We are called to be ambassadors of reconciliation (2 Cor 5:20). Technically, wherever an ambassador is, she is standing on the sovereign soil of her home country. So if the British ambassador is in line at a deli in Washington, D.C., she is standing on British soil. We are ambassadors of the kingdom of God with a sovereign mandate often at odds with a culture of violence and alienation. Our allegiance is not to a country but to a person: Jesus.

In May 2001, only a few months before the tragedies of 9/11 would escalate a wave of nationalism in churches across the United States, the Baptist World Alliance, a global fellowship of over 177,000 churches with 42 million members, issued the Berlin Declaration, a bold statement against nationalism. This declaration laments Baptist complicity in nationalism: "We confess that as Baptist Christians and Churches, we have often been complicit in this, [and have failed to] love the stranger, to speak and act decisively and to be peacemakers and reconcilers." Furthermore, it recognizes that "nationalism or adherence to a national ideology which exalt one nation over others are forms of idolatry and not compatible with Christian beliefs," and urges Baptists to "work for justice and peace for all, and to actively oppose war and violence as a means of settling national disputes and ethnic conflicts."[6]

To imagine a slow church is to trust that God has reconciled all things in Christ, to resist the worship of the nation and to embody our call to be peacemakers, bearing witness to God's reconciliation in Christ beginning in our own particular places.

CHURCH GROWTH AND THE HOMOGENEOUS UNIT PRINCIPLE

In chapter two, we got a glimpse of a kind of fragmentation that is embedded in the popular ideology of church growth. By applying the homogeneous unit principle and focusing on a very narrow demographic sector, we have demonstrated that it's possible to build extremely large churches. But at what cost? What is the cost to those who don't fit the particular demographic we've chosen as our homogeneous unit?

To achieve growth while maintaining homogeneity, megachurches draw their members from a very wide radius. What are the ecological costs of driving to a church community centered thirty minutes or more from our homes? What message do we convey to churches in and around our neighborhoods when we zip past them to go to distant churches that we deem more desirable? What is the cost to the megachurch in terms of the depth of its life together? How much life together can feasibly be shared by church members who live an hour or more from each other? When my (Chris's) wife and I first became a part of the Englewood Christian Church community, we lived about one mile from the church. Even at this relatively short distance, it was difficult to participate as actively in the life of the church as the people who lived within blocks of the building. The farther one lives from the locus of church activity the greater the inertia that must be overcome in order to participate.

The church growth movement is the most blatant expression of the McDonaldization of the church. South American theologian René Padilla is reported to have quipped that "Church Growth people assume that you can make Christians the way you make cars and sausages."[7] And like the industrialism of the nineteenth and twentieth centuries, there is a real sense in which the church growth movement has succeeded in some places, particularly in the North American suburbs. But we come back to the question, "At what cost?"

You can leverage the homogeneous unit principle to grow a huge church. You can use big screens and the latest technology, combined with the trendiest music and most exciting preachers, to give your church an attractive sheen. But what is the fruit that it produces? And what is the cost of the apparent success of megachurches to brother and sister churches in adjacent urban and older suburban areas? Statistics show that the vast majority of church growth under this model comes from "'switchers'—people who move from one church to another based on the perception and experience of the programming."[8]

In inner-city Indianapolis, I (Chris) see the deep wounds of neighborhoods that have been abandoned by churches and Christians who have fled for suburbia. When a church moves from one place to another, what impact does that have on neighbors who are left behind? What kind of witness does the church bear when it flees the challenges of a neighborhood rather than becoming engaged in them? Which do we prefer, the homogeneity of our congregations or God's reconciliation of all things? The church growth movement's emphasis on homogeneity seems to imply that it sets its sights on something less than God's reconciliation of all humanity and all creation.

POLITICAL PARTISANSHIP

I (John) grew up a diehard Republican. I listened to Rush Limbaugh during the day, tape-recorded it, and then listened to it again at night. I got so wrapped up in politics as a kid that doctors feared it was giving me ulcers. At the age of fourteen, I cried myself to sleep the night Bill Clinton was elected president. But later I switched parties, voting for John Kerry in the 2004 election and for Barack Obama in 2008. I noticed, however, that in conversations about important topics like gun control, immigration and civil rights, some of my conservative relatives would automatically dismiss anything I had to say on the grounds that I was a Democrat. Because the conversation was far more important to me than political identity, I happily re-registered as "unaffiliated." I took the conversation-killing card off the table. Now there is less ideological baggage as I find the common ground with relatives.

Political partisanship is another common fragmentation among churches and Christians in the United States—and one similar in form to nationalism. It afflicts Christians on both the right and left ends of the political spectrum. The issue isn't so much that they have aligned themselves with one particular party but that they have elevated political affiliation above their identity as followers of Christ and failed to cooperate toward the common good.

Most people who align themselves with the right or the left have rational theological explanations for their political orientation. The problem, as with all the sorts of fragmentation described here, is the failure to consider the larger picture. It's easy to think of reconciliation in the narrowest theological terms, but maybe a practical definition might be more useful: reconciliation is our capacity to talk and work with "the other" toward the common good. With this definition in mind, we see that Congress is in the throes of the worst kind of partisanship: Democrats and Republicans refuse to listen and work together.

The gulf between the two major parties has been expanding over the last several decades, a phenomenon Bill Bishop examines in his important 2008 book *The Big Sort: Why the Clustering of Like-Minded America Is Tearing Us Apart*. Bishop observes that "Americans have used wealth and technology to invent and secure places of minimal conflict. They spend more time with people like themselves. Politicians are sharply partisan, mirroring the homogeneity of the electorate."[9]

It is easy to dismiss partisanship as an idiosyncrasy of Washington, but to do so is to turn a blind eye toward the ways in which we as churches and individuals are affected by it. At the root of partisan struggles lies the issue of power, namely, who gets to control the direction of a nation (or state or municipality, etc.) It's helpful to contrast this partisan grappling for power with the example of Jesus. Although he was God, he emptied himself and didn't wield power in order to lord it over others. The tension of politics for God's people today is on the one hand to seek the health and common good of the *polis,* while on the other hand resisting the lust for power that is central to the identity of the political parties. Navigating this tension takes creativity and begins with our learning to be reconciled to our sisters and brothers in our local church communities.

One of the most exciting things that emerged in the 2012 presidential election season was the Election Day Communion movement. Founded by two Mennonites and an Episcopalian, the movement challenged congregations to join together on the evening of Election Day to share Communion together and to be reminded, in so doing, that regardless of our political affiliation we are one in Christ Jesus. One Mennonite pastor, whose church participated in celebrating Election Day Communion together, observed: "The level of rhetoric and discourse [in the election season] has been so divisive. I think it is important to remind believers that their identity is in Christ, and that we are called to unity and reconciliation. In my own church there are Republicans, Democrats and Independents. We are wanting to call people to remember that only in Jesus is there ultimate hope."[10]

BARRING CERTAIN PEOPLE FROM OUR CHURCHES

One final fragmentation that should be named is a church's unwillingness to extend welcome and hospitality to any particular group of people, especially on the basis of their race, ethnic origin, economic class or sexual orientation. Any theology that refuses to extend hospitality fails to consider God's love for and the reconciliation of all humanity. Martin Luther King Jr. famously observed that Sunday morning at eleven o'clock was the most segregated hour of the week. While there has been a hopeful movement toward multicultural churches since King's death, racism is still a major problem among Christians. The primary racism of today, however, is usually not the sort that bars people of a certain skin color from our churches, but rather the more subtle racism that compels our churches to move elsewhere when the racial (or economic) demographics of our neighborhoods begin to change.

The most divisive struggle in the church today relates to sexual orientation, an issue that has brought many large denominations close to the point of splitting. There are, of course, a host of complex questions being debated in churches and denominations around the world. Among them: Is homosexuality a sin? Is it what God intended for humanity? Are there certain forms (e.g., a covenanted, monogamous relationship) that are preferable to others? We don't have the space here to immerse ourselves in these questions, but even if a church thinks all forms of homosexuality are sinful, they must be mindful of the beam of sin and brokenness in their own eyes. They need to recognize that all people are created in the image of God and worthy of hospitality. Andrew Marin has done superb work in engaging and extending hospitality to the gay community and encouraging Christians to repent of their deep-rooted fear and hatred toward gays. At the close of his hugely important book, *Love Is an Orientation: Elevating the Conversation with the Gay Community*, Marin says:

We're not called to posit theories that support our assump-
tions. We're not called to speculate about genetics or developmental experiences or spiritual oppression in faceless groups
of other people. We're called to build bridges informed by
Scriptures and empowered by the Spirit. We're called to let a
just God be the God of his creation. We're called to let the
Holy Spirit whisper truth into each person's heart. And we're
called to show love unconditionally, tangibly, measurably.[11]

If we believe God is indeed reconciling all humanity and all creation, we must be willing to extend hospitality and open the gate
on the way toward reconciliation; no one should categorically be
barred from moving in this direction with us. We wish more
churches could follow in the footsteps of the self-described "ecu-
menical evangelical" Lasalle Street Church in urban Chicago,
which proclaims:

> At LaSalle Street Church, everyone is welcome. Regardless of
> your age, race, culture, gender, marital status, sexual orien-
> tation, your religious background, your disabilities, or your
> different abilities, you are welcome here. Whether you have
> money or not, whether you have a degree or not, whether you
> have a home or not, you are welcome here. LaSalle Street
> Church is committed to being a loving community of faith,
> built on the foundation of the Good News of Jesus Christ. We
> pray you will experience healing love and the full welcome of
> Christ in the time you spend with us.[12]

LAMENTING OUR FRAGMENTATION

Christianity has been plagued by fragmentation throughout its
history. Even the struggles between Jews and Gentiles dealt with at
length in the epistles of Paul were rooted in the failure to consider
the whole of God's work. Paul repeatedly challenged both Jews and

Gentiles to live peaceably together as the united people of God. Within a century of Paul's lifetime, however, the church had taken a sharp turn away from its Jewish roots, and it continued to fragment over the centuries: Constantinianism, anti-Protestantism, anti-Catholicism, racism, and so on. This atomistic way of thinking and acting is our heritage, the burden we bear, and it's not going away anytime soon. The different forms of fragmentation mentioned above reflect our continued failure to orient ourselves toward God's all-encompassing reconciliation. What would it look like for us to be an ecological people, a people ever mindful of God's reconciliation of all humanity and all creation? How do we embody a different way? A slow church begins with lament, or repentance, and then identifies practices that will help its community think and act ecologically.

To lament is to come alongside those who grieve, to sit with them (literally or figuratively) in the silence and to recognize there that in God's interconnected creation, their pain is our pain. We might, in the silence, consider how it is that we share in the same pain. To lament is not to offer words of comfort; it is not to try to fix the problem or to prevent it from ever happening again. Diving headlong into a debate about gun control, for instance, after a tragic shooting such as the ones in Aurora, Colorado, or Newtown, Connecticut, is not lament. Lament is the time for the hard work of searching our own souls, looking for the sorts of rebellion and violence that if untended could burst out in violence toward others. Thomas Merton once offered this poignant description of lament:

> Instead of hating the people you think are war-makers, hate the appetites and disorder in your own soul, which are the causes of war. If you love peace, then hate injustice, hate tyranny, hate greed—but hate these things in yourself, not in another.[13]

In their book *Reconciling All Things*, Chris Rice and Emmanuel Katongole describe lament as the means by which we unlearn speed, distance and innocence. As we are slowed by lament, we come to see not only how deeply broken we, and all creation, are but also that in Christ we have been given a way out of this huge mess. The way begins in our hearts and eventually leads to confession in our local congregation and then to the extension of grace and forgiveness by the church community. The journey of lament, though it may be initiated by an external event, proceeds from the personal through confession to forgiveness and restoration, ultimately serving to deepen the fellowship—from the Greek word *koinonia*, literally "common life"—of the congregation.

Lamentation is the beginning. We recognize and name the issue and seek to understand the many ways in which we are formed by it. We shine on it the compassionate light of Christ. This is especially important when the divides run deeper than our local faith communities—in our denominations or long-established church traditions. We often think of repentance as a complete break with the past. But the sorts of fragmentation we've described in this chapter are deeply embedded in the culture of our churches. They will not disappear overnight. We should expect change to come slowly, but we shouldn't give up hope or become cynical.

Wendell Berry's poem "The Wages of History"[14] carries wisdom that is particularly relevant to this conversation. On the surface, Berry is describing the way in which the land of his native Kentucky has been inattentively farmed, to such an extent that there is barely any soil left in which to raise crops. He contrasts the situation in Kentucky with the careful attention to the land given in places like Tuscany or Japan, where the hillsides have been terraced and preserved for many centuries. For Kentucky famers, the shortsightedness of past generations has now become a matter of life and death. They are "doomed, bound and doomed," Berry says, "to the repair of history or to death." Repentance, the poet goes on to say, requires sacrifice: the farmers must live "drawn out or nearly broken." The inattentive work of the past must be redone alongside the work of the present.

The tough road ahead of Kentucky farmers is not unlike the one we face in the Western church. Decades, if not centuries, of taking shortcuts have repelled many people from the faith and diminished the quality of our life together. The fragmentations described in this chapter are responsible for much of the damage—though certainly not all of it—and their effects run deep. Like the steep hillsides of Kentucky, it will take many, many years for these fractures to heal. In the meantime, those of us who recognize the damage must live sacrificially as we work both to care for the demands of the present and to begin the long work of healing past wounds.

Berry doesn't use the language of Christlikeness, but that's what comes through in his poem. Christ came both to restore Israel and to teach the community of twelve disciples who would take the message of God's reconciliation into all the world, to both Jews and Gentiles. We are called to take up our crosses and follow in the footsteps of Jesus, giving ourselves as "living sacrifices" (Rom 12:1) as we repent of the past and present sins of the church.

LIVING TOGETHER IN MORE HOLISTIC WAYS

As we lament our fragmented lives, we need to proactively adopt practices that are mindful of God's reconciling work. To begin with, we need to slow down our decision-making processes and consider broadly as we go what the ramifications of our decisions might be. There is much to be commended in practices like the Quaker tradition of consensus decision making, where everyone has a chance to reflect on the decision at hand and to speak into the process of making the decision. During the process of writing this book, my (John's) family and I began the process of engaging a clearness committee to help us through a complicated decision with a lot of moving parts: whether or not to move from our house four miles outside Silverton into Silverton proper and, if so, whether or not we should start some kind of intentional community or house of hospitality, and what part of town we should root ourselves in. In the case of our family, the discernment process was both shortened and fulfilled when we were invited to be part of a fledgling intentional community in the Danger Hill neighborhood of Silverton.

The clearness committee is a distinctly Quaker practice that has been around for 350 years. (Because the early Quakers didn't have leaders to hand down decisions from on high, they had to rely on the voice of the community and the promptings of the Holy Spirit.) Four or five people gather to help the discerner, who often prepares a document for the meeting that includes a statement of the issue at hand, its background and other pertinent details. Then the clearness committee meets for up to two hours, asking the discerner open and honest questions but also leaving plenty of room for silence. The atmosphere is quiet, unhurried and prayerful, and committee members are forbidden from offering advice. The process is also completely confidential. Even after the meeting has ended, the clearness process doesn't end. Says Parker Palmer, a Quaker educator, "The rest of us need simply to keep holding that person in the light, trusting the wisdom of his or her inner teacher."[15]

Palmer has written extensively about clearness committees, which he says free us from the pretense that we know what is best for the other person and the arrogant assumption that we are obliged to "save" each other. Instead, through listening, we create the conditions that allow a person to find his or her wholeness.

> If the spiritual discipline behind the clearness committee is understood and practiced, the process can become a way to renew community in our individualistic times, a way to free people from their isolation without threatening their integrity, a way to counteract the unhelpful excesses to which we sometimes take "caring," and a way to create space for the Spirit to move among us with healing and with power.[16]

We need to cultivate rich practices of discernment, where decisions are made not by a single person or a small group of leaders locked up in a boardroom, but by the community as a whole. Creation displays a deep and glorious diversity. It's no surprise then that God's reconciliation of creation will require a many-sided wisdom (Eph 3:9-10), which we've been given in the church.

As we repent of our stingy vision, we need to adopt practices that will help us think about the ramifications of our decisions over the long term. We can learn a lot from the Iroquois practice of seventh-generation thinking, which tried to discern what the outcomes of a decision might be not only for adults and children and grandchildren but for the seven (or more) generations to come:

> In all your efforts at law making, in all your official acts, self interest shall be cast into oblivion. . . . Look and listen for the welfare of the whole people and have always in view not only the present but also the coming generations, even those whose faces are yet beneath the surface of the ground—the unborn of the future nation. (The Constitution of the Iroquois Nations)[17]

How amazing would it be for churches to lead the way toward a culture where self-interest and immediate gratification were set aside in a Christlike fashion and seventh-generation decision making became commonplace?

A great deal of damage has been done in our churches and in our communities by our failure to be attentive to God's reconciliation of all things. As we embrace the complex interconnectedness of people and places, as we think more extensively about the ramifications of our decisions, and as we bring more and diverse voices to the table, the pace of our life together will inevitably slow. God, who is not in a hurry, has called us into a life that is attentive to God's reconciling work. Our impatience, our susceptibility to the temptations of individualism and McDonaldization, have, over the course of decades, distracted us from this calling. It's time for us to repent, to slow down and be ever mindful of God's all-encompassing mission of reconciliation.

CONVERSATION STARTERS

1. Name some of the fragmentations that exist in your congregation. Race? Age? Economic class? Political party? Where are the spaces in your life together where people on either side of any of these divides can actively engage with those on the opposite side—talking and working together and knowing each other first and foremost as brothers and sisters in Christ? How can you nurture more of these opportunities for healing and reconciliation to begin?

2. What is your congregational process for decision making? How do you ensure that as many people as possible can speak into the decision-making process if they so desire? How carefully do you examine the impact your decisions might have on your neighbors? On other churches? On the land or creation as a whole? Are there ways for people outside your congregation, who might have wisdom pertinent to a particular decision, to speak into your discernments?

6

Work

Cooperating with God's Reconciling Mission

Let this slow labor
bring light to earth

John Leax, "Prayer"

One of the first jobs I (John) had was working in a little country diner my mother owned in Gypsum, Kansas, population 365. The name on the Pepsi sign out front was simply "The Restaurant" (it was the only restaurant in town), and it was open for breakfast and lunch Monday through Friday and for supper on Friday nights. Some Friday nights it seemed like the entire town came to supper at the Restaurant—probably because the women making the food in the back, including my mom, were some of the best cooks around.

The Restaurant didn't really need my help. School was out for the summer, I wasn't a teenager yet, and I had four brothers at home; bringing one of us boys to work was a way for my mom to improve the odds that the house would still be standing when she got home. My job was to wash dishes, clear and clean tables, sweep the floor and walk the daily deposit to the bank down the street. For this I was paid a little money and given one of the Restaurant's "world-famous" cinnamon rolls. I ate my cinnamon roll around ten, when I could listen to the farmers who came in for their mid-morning cup of coffee. The farmers sat together at a long table, gossiping, complaining about the rain when it was raining, praying for rain when it was dry, speculating about the unfamiliar cars driving past, telling jokes and swapping stories. I already knew I was going to be a writer, but my experience working at the Restaurant, taking my breaks with those farmers during the dog days of summer, made me want to tell stories on behalf of rural Americans. It made me fiercely protective of flyover country and gave me an early glimpse of how a third place can become a "great good place"[1] that contributes to the health of a community. And it helped me see that work could be much more than a hateful necessity.

In contrast, my next job was at a McDonald's in Lincoln, Nebraska, when I was fifteen. I liked being there well enough, but only when I wasn't actually working. I wrote TV scripts (alas, unproduced) while I was working in the drive-through, memorized comedy routines, jokingly welcomed customers to Wendy's, flirted with female coworkers, and performed the chimneysweep scene from *Mary Poppins* with mops and deck brushes. Though I worked at the restaurant for three years, I left without developing any lasting friendships with customers or fellow "crew members," and without acquiring any useful skills (unless you count creating new and exciting sandwiches with cheese sauce squirted from a caulking gun). This was partly a lack of intentionality—pastor, professor and writer David Fitch goes to McDonald's every day, because that's where his neighbors are, and because "we might have to actually inhabit, engage and be present in order to bring justice to overwhelmingly large systems"[2]—but also because it is hard to connect at a deeply human level with others, or find meaning in your work, inside such a fast-paced, hyper-controlled and rationalized environment. This might be one reason why employee turnover in the fast food industry is close to 300 percent, the highest of any industry.

STRANGELY QUIET

Studs Terkel, the great radio broadcaster and Pulitzer Prize–winning author, reflected the tension that surrounds our modern experience of work. He begins his oral history of work with the extraordinary sentence, "This book, being about work, is by its very nature, about violence—to the spirit as well as the body." The physical and psychological violence to which Terkel refers is familiar to many of us. The anger and the accidents. The stress and humiliation. The deep dissatisfaction. That mercenary feeling that we've chosen money over meaning, that we've sold our sweat and swords to the highest bidder, sometimes at the expense of our own principles.

But then a couple paragraphs later, Terkel writes, "[This book] is about a search, too, for daily meaning as well as daily bread, for recognition as well as cash, for astonishment rather than torpor; in short, for a sort of life rather than a Monday through Friday sort of dying."[3] We recognize this too. Some of us have already experienced firsthand the savor of good work done well. Others are driven by hope that satisfying work is out there somewhere—because it just *has* to be. We know on a fundamental level that working for forty years at a job we hate, for the sake of maybe ten years of retirement during which we can do what we want, is a big gamble (since we might not live to retirement, or our retirement savings might not be there if we do) and maybe even a hatred of life, as Wendell Berry once said.

Work is such a complex, important and even intimate part of what it means to be human that it's surprising how little the American church has had to say about it in recent decades. Oh, every few years we'll hear from a business guru about "God the CEO" and "Jesus the Management Entrepreneur," but we don't often look at work from the ground up. How *relevant* can the church be to the day-to-day life of the world if it is silent on this topic? How *peculiar* can the church be if it lets society's dominant approaches to work go unexamined and, when necessary, unchallenged? Churches have particularly given a pass to the prevailing assumption of industrialism that work should be avoided as much as possible. G. K. Chesterton once quipped that "the Christian ideal has not been tried and found wanting; it has been found difficult and left untried."[4] Our contention, following Chesterton, is that when we take shortcuts for the sake of ease or efficiency, we dilute the vibrant joy of the gospel. In a culture dominated by convenience, our churches must recover the deep significance of good work.

Soulless work is one of the alienating effects of industrialization, along with unemployment, underemployment, low wages, child labor, the imposition of degraded work on degraded people and a ream of other consequences. But we can have a very different view of work, one that seeks a balance between taking work too seriously and not taking it seriously enough. Doing good work is one important way we respond as followers of Jesus to the work God is already doing around us.

THE SLOW CHURCH APPROACH TO WORK

M. Douglas Meeks cuts to the heart of things when he defines work this way: "Work is the power to answer with effort God's call to be God's economist in God's household."[5] Thus, the starting point for a slow church approach to work is recognition that we are not in control. Instead, we gratefully acknowledge that all heaven and earth is God's *household,* singing with the psalmist: "The earth is the LORD's, and everything in it, the world, and all who live in it" (Ps 24:1 NIV).

The concept of the household is an important one in Scripture. The word *oikos* ("house") is used over sixteen hundred times in the Septuagint. For the early Christian movement, the *oikos* was the starting point for all social, political, religious and economic activity.[6] Our own word "economics" comes from the Greek compound word *oikonomia,* which can be literally translated as "the law or management" (*nomos*) of the "household" (*oikos*). As we will explore further in chapter eight, God's economy, the law of God's household, is based not on scarcity but on abundance, not on accumulation but on livelihood, not on death but on life. For now it's enough to remind ourselves that we "are no longer strangers and aliens" but "fellow citizens with the saints and members of the household of God" (Eph 2:19 ESV). Good work should be fundamentally understood as cooperation with God. It is rooted in the work God has already done and is now doing, in our neighborhoods and in the world and in the church, while also looking ahead to the eschatological transformation of the new heaven and the new earth.

Meeks's definition is a much more expansive understanding of work than the way we most commonly use that word today, usually as a synonym for "gainful employment." The biggest problem with such a narrow usage is that it disregards the vital things done every day for no remuneration: for example, parenting, keeping house, volunteering for a local nonprofit or tending a home garden. If we reserve the word *work* for paid labor, it isn't long before we are ascribing levels of value to different kinds of work based on how much a person gets paid to do it. If the opposite were true—that is, if we tied salary to how important the work is by the standards of community flourishing—teachers, child care workers and farmers would be among the highest paid professions and not among the lowest; CEO salaries wouldn't be 209 times higher than the average worker's salary (up from 27 times higher in 1978); and the person hauling away the garbage would earn more than the person manufacturing it.

When I (John) was younger, I thought work was a result of the curse. My vision of Eden wasn't so different from the one depicted in a 1999 episode of *The Simpsons*. In "Three Bible Stories," Marge falls asleep during a sermon and dreams of the garden as a land of total peace, rest and sensual indulgence, a place where the lion lays down with the lamb and Homer can harmlessly peel strips of bacon from the belly of an obliging pig. I thought of paradise as perfect leisure, an idyllic life that came crashing down at the same time Adam and Eve were exiled from Eden for disobedience.

But I have come to realize how wrong I was in my theological understanding of work. Work isn't a result of the curse. Humankind is made in the image of God, who worked for six days and then rested on the seventh. In the first creation narrative, God makes man and woman and tells them to subdue the earth and have dominion over it, both of which imply work. The second creation narrative is more explicit. God forms the man out of dust from the ground and breathes life into his nostrils. God plants the garden in Eden and then puts the man into the garden "to work it and take care of it" (Gen 2:15 NIV). Miroslav Volf says "working" in the garden and "keeping it" (or taking care of it) aren't separate kinds of activities, but two aspects of all human work. "All work," he writes, "must have not only a productive but also a protective aspect. Economic systems must therefore be integrated into given biological systems of ecological interdependence."[7] It's worth noting too that both creation narratives are clear that good work is done in cooperation with, and with an eye toward, the broader creaturely community.

After the Fall, however, work takes on the character of toil and becomes an economic necessity. God says to Adam in Genesis 3:17 and 19, "Cursed is the ground because of you; in toil you shall eat of it all the days of your life. . . . By the sweat of your face you shall eat bread." (If we need another reason to walk gently on the land, here it is: the curse is our fault.)

There is no biblical evidence that work itself is a curse. Zechariah's vision of the new Jerusalem does not depict a future free from work but rather a future in which work is once again perfectly situated in the abundance of God (8:10-12). We find throughout Scripture stories of God equipping God's people for God's work. We see this in the Old Testament, in the story of the workers who had been filled with "divine spirit, with ability, intelligence, and knowledge in every kind of craft. . . . I [God] have given skill to all the skillful, so that they may make all that I have commanded you" (Ex 31:3-4, 6). And we see it in the New Testament:

> Now there are varieties of gifts, but the same Spirit; and there are varieties of services, but the same Lord; and there are varieties of activities, but it is the same God who activates all of them in everyone. To each is given the manifestation of the Spirit for the common good. (1 Cor 12:4-7)

This passage indicates just how spiritually devastating dehumanizing work can be. One ancient standard of economic justice was a person's freedom to fully utilize their God-given faculties. While we should be careful not to romanticize the distant past—after all, this vocational freedom was, in many societies, available only to a very limited class of free people—it's useful to keep in mind work's ideal: work that engages the whole person, often in collaboration with others, for the sake of the flourishing of the whole community.

ADAM SMITH AND THE DIVISION OF LABOR

How has work come to be so meaningless? Western understandings of work have changed over the last three centuries, a story that unfolds in parallel with the rise of industrialization.

Adam Smith (1723–1790) put work at the center of individual and social life. Smith is the father of modern economics and the patron saint of modern capitalism, but he didn't consider work in terms of human dignity, only its usefulness.[8] The market, he believed, is a machine that runs according to inherent laws and should be left alone. That machine is attuned to the consumer. The purpose of work is production, and the sole purpose of all production, said Smith, is consumption. Thus, work is a means to an end. People endure it because it affords them the power to buy things and pay for services. So on a macro level work is a positive force, because the most important source of an empire's wealth is human labor. But on an individual level work is a negative, something to generally be avoided if one can afford it.

Smith believed that the key to reducing the workload, eliminating the human factor, improving the lot of every social class and propelling society forward is *division of labor.* Division of labor assigns discrete parts of a manufacturing process to different people in order to improve efficiency and increase productivity. The example Smith uses in the first chapter of *The Wealth of Nations* (1776) is the manufacturing of pins, which in a factory Smith visited was broken into eighteen distinct operations. An unskilled workman working alone couldn't make twenty pins in one day, Smith said; but ten "very poor" men in a factory, with only a casual knowledge of the machinery and each performing two or three distinct operations, could make up to forty-eight thousand pins a day.

According to Smith, this division of labor shapes us as *individuals.* There are philosophers, taxi cab drivers, baristas, schoolteachers and factory workers. What separates these individuals is less a difference of natural talents than it is differences of custom, education, habit and opportunity. The division of labor also shapes us as a *society,* because the philosopher and cabbie and factory worker are interdependent on one another.

One of the severe drawbacks of the division of labor is its alienating character. Miroslav Volf, in his book *Work in the Spirit,* describes alienation as the "significant discrepancy between what work should be as a fundamental dimension of human existence and how it is actually performed and experienced by workers."[9] Workers are exploited. They become estranged from themselves and their tasks, which are often repetitive, uninteresting and unsatisfying. The work can be dehumanizing and, as Volf says, an assault on human creativity. What's interesting is that Adam Smith recognized this alienation. Smith writes:

The man whose whole life is spent in performing a few simple
operations . . . has no occasion to exert his understanding, or
to exercise his invention. . . . He naturally loses, therefore, the
habit of such exertion, and generally becomes as stupid and
ignorant as it is possible for a human creature to become.[10]

In the end, Smith regretted the alienation that accompanies the
division of labor, but he accepted a certain amount of it as the cost
of doing business in an "improved and civilized society."

TAYLORISM AND THE ASSEMBLY LINE

The division of labor produced an enormous amount of wealth, but
its inherent alienation also gave rise to powerful, dehumanizing
systems that still shape our world. One such system is scientific
management, sometimes referred to as Taylorism, in honor of its
founder, Frederick W. Taylor (1856–1915). An inventor and en-
gineer, Taylor developed methods of subdividing the workplace
into minute components that could be quantified, evaluated, standardized and controlled, all with the goal of making the office or
factory more efficient. Taylor didn't trust workers to use their own
initiative. Under scientific management, he said, "the 'initiative' of
the workmen" is obtained through absolute uniformity. Managers
are tasked with gathering all of the traditional knowledge possessed
by the workers, classifying and tabulating that knowledge, and then
reducing it to rules, laws and formulas. Taylor timed workers with
a stopwatch, analyzed every motion to determine which were essential, and eliminated wasted motions and wasted time. Workers
were more productive when they followed this robotlike routine.

It would be a mistake to think that scientific management is just
a quaint relic of the late nineteenth and early twentieth centuries.
Management aficionado Peter Drucker named Taylor, Sigmund
Freud and Charles Darwin the seminal makers of the modern world.
Taylor's monograph, *The Principles of Scientific Management* (1911),

was the first business bestseller. V. I. Lenin told Soviet workers to experiment with "every scientific and progressive suggestion of the Taylor system." When workers couldn't replicate Taylor's production targets they were sent to the Gulag. Taylor was also hugely influential on Henry Ford, and he worked with the automaker to perfect the first assembly line. Scientific management and the assembly line, as will be obvious, are precursors to McDonaldization.

Taylorism is profoundly dehumanizing for at least two reasons. First, it treats people as expendable. Once the traditional knowledge has been extracted from a skilled worker and codified into rules and formulas and essential motions, "unskilled" workers can be trained just enough to be plugged into preexisting slots. Because workers do very few tasks, most of their real skills and abilities remain unused.[11] There is no room for creativity; innovation is not encouraged. Second, scientific management separates "head" work from "hand" work.[12] In the old system, all the planning had been done by the worker, on the basis of personal experience. Taylor believed that planning must now be done by management.

Matthew B. Crawford writes in his excellent book *Shop Class as Soulcraft* that "wherever the separation of thinking from doing has been achieved, it has been responsible for the degradation of work."[13] People initially resisted Taylorism and Ford's assembly line. Early in his career, when he was first developing the principles of scientific management, Taylor used both carrots and sticks (including fines and firings) to double the productivity of skilled machinists working at a Philadelphia steelworks. But the machinists were unhappy with the changes, and they grew hostile toward Taylor. In 1911, workers at a government arsenal in Watertown, Massachusetts, went on strike to protest Taylor's methods, leading to a grueling, months-long Congressional committee hearing on scientific management. When Henry Ford first introduced the assembly line in 1913, the company had to hire 963 people for every 100 empty positions. Workers just walked out. "This would seem to be a crucial moment in the history of political economy," writes Crawford. "Evidently, the new system provoked natural revulsion. Yet, at some point, workers became habituated to it."[14] As we will see, one of the roles of the slow church in a McDonaldized society is to help people recognize and pursue good work over bad work.

THE McDONALDIZATION OF WORK

In 1958, a McDonald's executive named Fred L. Turner (later the cofounder of Hamburger University) compiled a training manual that was seventy-five pages long. Internally this manual was called "the Bible," and it prescribed how everything was to be done, including how many rows of burgers should be placed on the grill (six) and how thick the french fries should be (0.28 inches). Today, "the Bible" has ten times as many pages, weighs four pounds and continues to dictate every aspect of operations inside a McDonald's restaurant. This is an example of how, in a McDonaldized society, the workplace can become a large-scale nonhuman technology.

We tend to think of technology as machines, equipment, tools, gadgets, electronics and devices. But the concept is actually much broader than that. Our word "technology" comes from a compound Greek word meaning the systematic treatment of an art or craft. Technology can thus also include rules, regulations, materials and skills. The sociologist George Ritzer says that technologies "encompass not only the obvious, such as robots and computers, but also the less obvious, such as the assembly line, bureaucratic rules, and manuals prescribing accepted procedures and techniques."[15] Human technologies (a hammer or screwdriver) are controlled by people. Nonhuman technologies control people. Scientific management, the Burger King drive-through, assembly instructions for an Ikea bookshelf—these are all nonhuman technologies. So, for that matter, are many modern workplaces. As Frederick Taylor put it: "In the past the man has been first; in the future the system must be first."

One of the characteristics of industrialization has been the pro-liferation of nonhuman technologies that increasingly order our homes, jobs, entertainments and churches. The fast food industry is only the most obvious example. We could just as easily look at nonhuman technology in the airline industry, medicine, the mil-itary, the office, customer service or retail shopping. We even heard about a large church near West Palm Beach that has an operating manual for its worship team.

The church in Florida is an extreme illustration of how some of the most dehumanizing aspects of McDonaldization have crept into our churches. Members of the worship team must wear black, must not be overweight, must stand in one spot on stage, and must not raise their hands or do or wear anything to draw attention to them-selves. Would-be worship team members are compelled to check their individuality at the door. Automatons are welcome. We're re-minded of Burger King's Rule 17, which states that employees must "Smile at all times"—a royal edict both creepy and cruel, because it is emotionally false and physically impossible. What it all really boils down to, of course, is control.

Though it is beyond the scope of this book to explore in detail, it's worth considering whether there may be a connection between a rationalized operating manual like the McDonald's "Bible" de-scribed above and the way some people approach the actual Bible. The McDonald's "Bible" tells an employee how to act and move in every situation, in every place in the restaurant. Some people ap-proach the Bible the same way, looking to Scripture as a compre-hensive roadmap that should lead them through life with a fair amount of certainty and efficiency. We wonder, though, if this asks the Bible to be something it was never intended to be. The Jews didn't look to the Hebrew Scriptures primarily to find answers but to help them know the right questions to ask. Scripture was the starting point for a lifelong conversation with God that took place within the context of the larger community. For both of us, Scripture is more of a compass than a roadmap. The compass points to Jesus as True North. That's where the journey—the conversation, the relationship—starts.

NURTURING GOOD WORK IN OUR CHURCHES

So how do our churches begin to be transformed in the ways that we think about work—from meaninglessness to meaningful, rooted in the mission of God? Dorothy Sayers, who wrote brilliantly about work in the *The Mind of the Maker,* in several essays and even in her detective stories, hit the nail on the head when she said that seeing work as a consequence of the fall saps work of its sacramental value. "The whole of Christian doctrine centers round the great paradox of redemption, which asserts that the very pains and sorrows by which fallen man is encompassed can become instruments of his salvation, if they are accepted and transmuted by love."[16] What are some practical ways in which the neighborhood *ekklesia*—local expressions of the household of God—can begin to reclaim work as an expression and instrument of God's *shalom*? There are too many to list here, and every local gathering of Jesus followers should come up with strategies that arise from their own particular contexts, but here are a few of our ideas to get the conversation going.

1. *Help people recognize and prefer good work over bad work.* The most important distinction in our culture isn't between white-collar work and blue-collar work; it's between bad work and good work. (In fact, we think taking good work seriously will remove some of the prejudices against manual labor and the trades.) Bad work is meaningless, stultifying and exploitative; it puts the system before the person and lays waste to the earth. Good work is good for the community and good for the one doing it. It is modestly scaled, situated and can be done well. As has been noted by E. F. Schumacher and Wendell Berry, among others, the metaphysics of materialism is incapable of helping us distinguish good work from bad.

The church should come alongside people who are asking questions about vocation and work, because notions of work are too closely tied to the ultimate questions that materialism is ill-equipped to answer: Who am I? Who am I with? How did I get here? What am I supposed to do? One of the primary functions of the *ekklesia* should be to help people discern their gifts, develop those gifts and exercise those gifts through cooperative work with God—whether that's at home, in the church, in the community, in a job or as a volunteer.

2. *Explore the possibilities (and limitations) of work as worship.* The opening question of the Westminster Shorter Catechism asks, "What is the chief end of man?" The answer: "Man's chief end is to glorify God, and to enjoy Him forever." Work is not the chief end of man.[17] If we want to radically transform our families and communities, there are few better starting points than to acknowledge the truth of that last statement, consider its implications and adjust our lives accordingly. At the same time, good work done well *can* be a form of worship, if we mean it to be. God is radically immanent even in the most mundane tasks. Kathleen Norris points out in her little book *The Quotidian Mysteries* that our word *menial* derives from a Latin word meaning "to remain" or "to dwell in a household." It is a word about connections and household ties, she says. Later Norris suggests that what strikes us as "the ludicrous attention to detail in the book of Leviticus, involving God in the minutiae of daily life—all the cooking and cleaning of a people's life—might be revisioned as the very love of God. A God who cares so much as to desire to be present to us in everything we do."[18] Work is hard. It can be taxing. And it is always there. But even in the midst of the daily grind we can offer our work back to God for God's glory. At that point false distinctions between "secular" work and "sacred" work begin to crumble.

3. *Champion work-related justice.* It's remarkable how many of today's most urgent social injustices are related to work. According to the International Labor Organization, there are more than 215

million children between the ages of five and fourteen in the work-force worldwide. About half of those kids are working full time to help support their impoverished families. Approximately 126 million children are subject to the worst forms of child labor, including slavery or other forms of forced labor, drug trafficking, prostitution, involvement in armed conflict and work in hazardous environments.[19] Needless to say, these are children who, in a different context, would look very much like our own sons and daughters, our younger brothers and sisters, our neighbors. Not for Sale, an organization dedicated to fighting human trafficking around the world, estimates that there are more than 30 million slaves in the world today, more than at any other point in human history. And human trafficking is not just happening halfway around the world. It's happening in our own cities and towns. Portland, Oregon, for example, is frequently cited as one of the most progressive and livable cities in the nation, but it has been confronted in recent years with evidence that it has become a regional hub for sex trafficking. The community is starting to respond.

Communities of faith can initiate weeks-long projects that help educate their people about the ways in which the issues of child labor and human trafficking hit home. (Mark Scandrette describes one such project in *Practicing the Way of Jesus*.[20]) Churches can also help prevent work-related injustices by providing services to local runaway and homeless teenagers, refugees, and undocumented workers, speaking out at town hall meetings and at the local chamber of commerce, and using media and the arts to tell the stories of real people harmed by abusive labor. Churches can also help hold corporations accountable. The site free2work.org tells "the tale of the barcode," providing customers with information on how companies are or are not addressing forced and child labor. Anti-Slavery International, a British charity founded in 1839, has an interactive map at productsofslavery.org that depicts slavery in the supply chain.

4. Recognize the human resources within our congregations and leverage them in the reconciling work of the kingdom. The scriptural story emphasizes that God is reconciling all things in creation. Having been called into this work as church communities, every member of the body of Christ has skills that can be leveraged. Educators in all kinds of schools, from daycare centers to graduate schools, can help us create learning environments that are beneficial to the well-being of our places. Builders, electricians and plumbers all have trades that can be utilized to help our places flourish. People with business and financial skills can help create needed jobs and can pursue financing needed for kingdom work. Doctors and nurses have knowledge and skills that can help us live more healthfully. Even lawyers can be beneficial to help our churches navigate the legal landscape with the shrewdness of serpents and the innocence of doves.

What if our churches became clearinghouses for good work in our neighborhoods, facilitating connections between employers looking for good workers and good workers looking for good jobs? What if our church communities became incubators of small businesses, nonprofits and volunteer associations built on the assets that are already in our community, waiting to be nurtured and to grow?

In her challenging book *Kingdom Calling,* Amy Sherman describes the movement of local churches orchestrating the skills and talents of their members for the reconciling work of the kingdom in their particular places as "vocational stewardship." Sherman urges churches to equip their members to recognize and use the broad range of their skills and talents (not just a limited range of "spiritual gifts") in helping their places to mature and flourish into healthy communities. At my (Chris's) church, vocational stewardship has meant starting businesses around the beneficial skills of its members, including my experiences in publishing/bookselling. It has also meant connecting people in the congregation with other neighborhood nonprofit and for-profit groups that could use their skills. With the assumption that everyone has talents that God wants to use for the kingdom, we get to know our members and their God-given gifts and then watch for opportunities for them to use and deepen their skills in ways that benefit the common good of our neighborhoods.

CONVERSATION STARTERS

1. What spaces does your church have in its life together for people to talk about and reflect theologically on the work they do? How does your congregation strengthen the bonds between the daily work of your members and the mission of the church in your place?

2. What gifts and skills do people in your congregation have that they are willing to make available for the reconciling work of the kingdom?

3. How can you connect people with particular skills that would benefit your neighborhood and empower people to begin exploring how they can use their gifts together in this way?

7

Sabbath

The Rhythm of Reconciliation

*When we become a Sabbath people, we give
one of the most compelling witnesses to the world
that we worship a God who desires our collective joy and good.
We give concrete expression to an authentic faith that is working to
deflate the anxious and destructive pride that supposes we have to
"do it all" by ourselves and through our own effort.*

Norman Wirzba, *Living the Sabbath*

Atop a high butte in Marion County, Oregon, about five miles from my (John's) house, there is a Benedictine monastery called Mt. Angel Abbey. On a clear day it is possible to sit on a bench next to the monastery's retreat house and look out over hundreds of square miles of Willamette Valley farmland known for its hops, wine grapes, berries and Christmas trees. Mount Angel has become for me what the nineteenth-century Swiss monks who built it must have intended it to be: a hilltop refuge, imbued with the spirit of those great Benedictine watchwords: *peace* and *hospitality*. I sometimes think of the abbey as a kind of lighthouse that has been pulsing through the Oregon rain and fog for more than 130 years, as the monks daily chant the psalms, worship, welcome strangers and pray for the world.[1]

There is another way I think of Mt. Angel Abbey, and it's captured in the beautiful Spanish word *querencia,* sometimes translated as the "haunt of wild hearts." The American writer Barry Lopez describes *la querencia* as a place on the ground from which one draws strength of character. Mt. Angel Abbey, where I am an oblate novice, is my *querencia.* It's the place I go to gather myself, to sing and pray and read, to catch my breath, to soak in silence, and sometimes to just sit on the abbey benches and look out over the valley I have come to love. I always seem to leave the monastery a little bit stronger, ready to charge (or at least limp) back down the hill into my workaday life.

Sabbath is also a kind of *querencia,* a day set aside that gives shape to our character and identity. Whereas the monastery is a place on the ground from which I draw strength, the sabbath is a place in time where we reconnect with God, who is the wellspring of all vitality. The great Jewish rabbi, philosopher and theologian Abraham Joshua Heschel wrote in his classic work *The Sabbath* about an "architecture of time" that stands in contrast to our preoccupation with the stuff of space. The sabbath is a reminder that time is "eternity in disguise" and that we belong to eternity. The architecture of time is built on every uniquely precious and sacred hour, for it is only in the present moment—*now . . . now . . . now*—that God dispenses God's provision, grace, beauty and wonder.

THE WORLD OF TOTAL WORK

In the early years of the twentieth century a German sociologist named Max Weber published *The Protestant Work Ethic and the Spirit of Capitalism,* an influential book that looked at the symbiotic relationship between modern capitalism and Protestantism, especially Calvinism. Modern capitalism is focused on the pursuit of profit. Weber argued that the perceived virtue of profit-seeking could be traced, in part, back to the Calvinist doctrine of double predestination—the belief that God has foreordained everything that will happen: both those who will be saved and those who will be damned. None of the Catholic consolations—priest, church or sacrament—were available to assuage the anxiety of Puritans faced with the ultimate question, "Elect or reprobate?"[2] So, according to Weber, they started looking to worldly prosperity—hard work, frugality, the generation of wealth through investment—as a sign of their election.

Weber believed that these values had, over time, taken root in the Western world and achieved a relative autonomy from Calvinist theology. He further believed that the country in which "the pursuit of gain" had become most stripped of its religious and ethical dimensions was the United States. Though we can see shades and mutations of Weber's Protestant ethic in today's prosperity gospel, the idea has been further secularized in the last hundred years. The virtue of frugality has been replaced by a debt-enabled addiction to consumption. And the Protestant work ethic has come close to giving us a world of "total work."[3]

We do come close to worshiping work in the United States. Eighty-six percent of American men and 67 percent of American women work more than forty hours a week. The Japanese have a word, karoshi, meaning "death by overwork," but, according to the International Labour Organization, Americans work 137 more hours per year than Japanese workers, 260 more hours per year than the British and 499 more hours per year than the French. We don't work to live; we live to work. The only one of the Ten Commandments we publicly brag about breaking is the one about remembering the sabbath and keeping it holy, and yet we are never given any indication (in the Old Testament or New Testament) that forsaking the sabbath is any more or less justifiable than murder, theft and adultery.

Severe overwork is not just a problem for people in so-called secular vocations. According to a 2010 study by LifeWay Research, 42 percent of full-time pastors work sixty or more hours per week, often at the expense of family, time spent in prayer and personal devotions.[4] Nor is this anything new. Thomas Merton wrote nearly fifty years ago about overwork as "a pervasive form of contemporary violence" that can undermine a well-meaning peace activist's calling:

> The rush and pressure of modern life are a form, perhaps the most common form, of its innate violence. To allow oneself to be carried away by a multitude of conflicting concerns, to surrender to too many demands, to commit oneself to too many projects, to want to help everyone in everything is to succumb to violence. More than that, it is cooperation in violence. The frenzy of the activist neutralizes his work for peace. It destroys his own inner capacity for peace. It destroys the fruitfulness of his own work, because it kills the root of inner wisdom which makes work fruitful.[5]

SABBATH ECONOMICS

Sabbath is an obvious rebuke to a culture—and even a church culture!—that prides itself on its busyness, scorns leisure as laziness and boasts that we'll sleep when we're dead. We see throughout Scripture the economic and social subversiveness of a sabbath ethic characterized by abundance, self-restraint and solidarity.[6] The first time we encounter the word "sabbath" (Hebrew, *shabat*) is in Exodus 16. God's people have been delivered from the slavery and oppression of Pharaoh's imperial economy. But as they wander in the wilderness, the people of Israel start grumbling against their leaders, Moses and Aaron. They say they would rather be enslaved in Egypt than die of hunger in the desert. "If only we had died by the hand of the LORD in the land of Egypt, when we sat by the fleshpots and ate our fill of bread; for you have brought us out into this wilderness to kill this whole assembly with hunger" (16:3).

God uses this as an opportunity to demonstrate God's provision and abundance. God gives the Israelites daily bread in the form of manna, which is described as being white and flaky and tasting of honey wafers. The Israelites ate manna for forty years. Six days a week, God sent bread from heaven. On the sixth day the Israelites gathered a double portion of food, because the seventh day was "a day of solemn rest, a holy sabbath to the LORD" (Ex 16:23).

Ched Myers, in his excellent book *The Biblical Vision of Sabbath Economics,* describes three important lessons God is teaching in this passage. These lessons are economic, but they are also ecological; they guide us into a life that is attentive to God's work of reconciling all things.

First, God's people learn the lesson of *enough.* God tells the people to gather just enough manna to get them through the day. Whether someone gathered too much or too little, it all came out the same, because "whoever gathered much had nothing left over, and whoever gathered little had no lack" (Ex 16:18 ESV). Compare this to the disparity in wealth between the global rich and the global poor. In 2000, the wealthiest 1 percent of the world's adults owned 40 percent of its assets. The richest 10 percent controlled 85 percent of global wealth. In the United States, income inequality is now as bad as it has been since the Great Depression, resembling that of developing countries. As individuals and families, we need to be asking tough questions about when we've reached enough. How much money do we need in our bank account or 401k? When are our homes nice enough? Our cars? How full do our closets need to be? We need to ask similar questions for our faith communities. What does "enough" look like for Silverton Friends Church and Englewood Christian Church and your church? Learning the lesson of enough forms us in a way that we are less inclined to jeopardize the lives and well-being of other humans and creatures by greedily taking too much.

Second, God teaches God's people the value of *redistribution*. As we will see in chapter eight, wealth and power in Egypt were defined by surplus accumulation. During the famine, the people of Egypt, including the people of Israel who were under the protection of Joseph, had to put up everything they owned for collateral in order to gain access to the grain silos of the imperial economy. Eventually the only thing they had left to barter was their own freedom. In contrast, God says the desert manna shouldn't be stored up. In fact, it was impossible to stockpile manna for profit or protection; manna left over the next morning became foul and bred worms. Ched Myers says that "Israel is enjoined to keep wealth *circulating* through strategies of redistribution, not *concentrating* through strategies of accumulation."[7] (It's also worth remembering that the first organized structure created by the new church in Acts 2 and 4 was a system of distribution that ended economic need among followers of the Way.) Redistribution teaches us to grow deeper in the reconciling economy of God in which God provides abundantly for us in order that we might share abundantly with others.

A Sunday school class at my (John's) church recently began experimenting with the implications of sabbath economics. For several weeks, each of us chose an area of our life where we could practice enough. One family chose to eat oatmeal for breakfast for a time, at a cost of just twenty-seven cents per person. Another cut out fancy coffee drinks. One man decided to take the bus to work two days a week instead of driving his car. After the experiment had concluded, we collected the money we had saved and discussed what we should do with it. Rather than give the cash to a charity, we decided to keep the money circulating through the church body. We knew of an older woman who couldn't afford to hire a skilled handyman to do some repairs on her house. And we knew of a skilled handyman in the church who was looking for more work. Presto!

The third lesson God teaches the Israelites is *sabbath faith and discipline*. As the Bible scholar Richard H. Lowery puts it, "Sabbath observance requires a leap of faith, a firm confidence that the world will continue to operate benevolently for a day without human labor, that God is willing and able to provide enough for the good life. Sabbath promises seven days of prosperity for six days of work."[8] Sabbath thus teaches us to abandon the prevailing wisdom of the world and to trust that God is indeed at work reconciling creation.

Later in the book of Exodus, we see the sabbath week extended to the sabbath year: every seventh year, the Israelites are told to "let [the land] rest and lie fallow, so that the poor of your people may eat; and what they leave the wild animals may eat" (Ex 23:10-11). It's also a year of canceling debts (Deut 15). In Leviticus 25, the sabbath year is extended to the sabbath's sabbath. Every fifty years the structures of accumulation and domination are upended by releasing each community member from debt (25:35-42), returning land to its original owners (25:13, 25-28), freeing slaves (25:47-55) and reminding Israel that the land belongs to God (25:23) and that they are an exodus people who must never return to a system of slavery (25:42).

In many of these same passages, we also find gleaning laws that allow the poor to have access to a field's produce. Farmers were forbidden to go back through their field a second time; instead, they were supposed to leave anything that had fallen and to leave the crops on the edge of the field. We recently heard about the Society of St. Andrew, a modern-day gleaning organization that salvages produce from American farms—food that would otherwise be left to rot in the fields—and delivers it to shelters, food banks and other charitable agencies. Not only does this help provide nutritious, farm-fresh produce to the poor, it also helps reduce the estimated ninety-six billion pounds of preconsumer food that annually goes to waste in the United States. Other people we know glean by collecting and giving away all their pocket change, by rounding up to the next dollar when calculating a tip and by "upcycling"—that is, repurposing old materials and products into something new and useful. Two artists in my (John's) church—one a metalworker, the other a woodworker—upcycle found materials to create beautiful works of art for the church. They have taken old wooden beams, sheet metal, tin and brass, conduit and other discarded items from construction sites to create a cross used for liturgy during Holy Week, a panorama of the foothills above Silverton, and a striking espresso bar where lattes and mochas are made before church (using hand-roasted beans, of course).

As we see in Genesis, Joseph was clearly set aside by God to save the lives of many thousands of people who were going to be hit hard by famine. But the economic centralization he initiated in Egypt also put in place the economic preconditions for Israel's future slavery. This is a reminder that "economic miracles" (in the words of M. Douglas Meeks) sometimes have unintended consequences. This is one rationale behind sabbath and Jubilee: to systematically dismantle the unintended consequences of economic miracles.

The prophet Isaiah seemed to be writing about the Jubilee year in Isaiah 61:

> The spirit of the Lord GOD is upon me,
>   because the LORD has anointed me;
> he has sent me to bring good news to the oppressed,
>   to bind up the brokenhearted,
> to proclaim liberty to the captives,
>   and release to the prisoners;
> to proclaim the year of the LORD's favor. (vv. 1-2)

This passage from Isaiah was Jesus' inauguration speech at the beginning of his ministry. When he finished reading it in the synagogue, he rolled up the scroll and sat back down. Luke 4 says that the eyes of everyone in the synagogue were fixed on him. Then

Jesus said, "Today this scripture has been fulfilled in your hearing" (Lk 4:21).

Sabbath and Jubilee had been a part of the fabric of the cosmos since the first week of creation, but here Jesus was announcing the Jubilee kingdom of God. St. Gregory the Great declares, "For us, the true Sabbath is the person of our Redeemer, our Lord Jesus Christ."[9] Sabbath and Easter become intertwined, with Sunday—the day most often associated with sabbath in the Christian tradition—often recognized as a "little Easter." As we will see, sabbath is made for humankind (Mk 2:27) because humankind was made for God—and the Son of Man (Jesus) is Lord of them both.

EXPERIMENTING WITH SABBATH DELIGHT

Over six days, God created day and night, the dome of sky, earth and its vegetation, the sun and moon and stars, the sea creatures and every winged bird, the wild animals, the cattle of every kind, "everything that creeps upon the ground" (Gen 1:25) and humankind. God saw everything God had made and it was very good.

The Bible says that on the seventh day God "finished the work that he had done, and he rested on the seventh day from all the work that he had done. So God blessed the seventh day and hallowed it, because on it God rested from all the work he had done in creation" (Gen 2:1-3). Thus we see at the very beginning of human history God inaugurates a basic rhythm of good work and rest, both of which are characterized by deep pleasure. It's almost as if the work of creation is not complete until the creation of work's ceasing.

We often assume that humans are the apex of the first week, but this isn't so. Though humans are given dominion over the earth, to protect and nurture it for its flourishing and our own, the pinnacle of creation was not humanity but sabbath rest (*menuha*). "After the six days of creation—what did the universe still lack? *Menuha.* Came the Sabbath, came *menuha,* and the universe was complete."[10]

Menuha is much more than a lack of activity. It implies peace, harmony, joy, celebration and delight. Dan Allender, a Christian therapist and writer, has written our favorite description of *menuha*:

> In many ways, God's rest on the seventh day of creation is paralleled by the birthing process and the period after birth, when the labor is finished yet the bonding begins. The mother and father gaze endlessly at their child, who is distinct from the parents because she is no longer merely in the mind and the womb of the mother, but external and separate. She is no longer solely in the imagination or deep in the womb; she is finally released to be held in the arms of the parent. This attachment brings mother and child into a bond that, if secure, will last through thick and thin, heartache and loss, and provide the child with an assurance that all will be well.[11]

Sabbath, then, becomes for us the day in which we pause our striving and start abiding. Far from a legalistic requirement, sabbath is an exercise in radical grace: in the midst of our sin and brokenness, God loves us. Our creator God looks down at us with absolute love; we set aside the sabbath to meet that gaze. Sabbath is the "animating heart" of life, as Norman Wirzba puts it. "To forget or deny Sabbath is thus to withhold our lives from their most authentic purposes in God." Refocusing on God can help us bring all our endeavors into realignment with their "all-encompassing, eternal objective, which is to participate in the life of God forever."[12]

Norman Wirzba and Dan Allender have both written essential books on what it can look like for twenty-first-century Christians to live the sabbath, and both talk about delight as one of the key characteristics of sabbath practice. (Urging his readers to experiment with the sabbath, Allender encourages us to ask, simply, "What would I do for a twenty-four-hour period of time if the only criteria was to pursue my deepest joy?") But they also acknowledge that delight can be scary. It takes faith to cease our striving, to trust that God promises seven days of provision for six days of work and to meet God's gaze. We know we haven't done anything to deserve this level of loving attention. Borrowing a metaphor from C. S. Lewis, we feel safer making mud pies in a slum than taking a holiday by the sea. "To consider what delights us is to stand accused by the countless moments of onerous obligation and unfulfilled dreams," writes Allender. "Instead, we would rather settle for distraction than open our hearts to what seems beyond our wildest dreams. We have learned to manage our disappointment with God, and we don't want our desire for delight to seduce us again."[13]

Earlier in the chapter I (John) mentioned that a Sunday school class at my church had begun experimenting with sabbath economics. That same group experimented with sabbath delight as well, both as individuals and as families. We came back together after a few weeks to recount our experiences and to encourage and learn from each other. My family felt strongly that the areas in which we had ceded too much ground to counterfeit pleasures were related to food and technology. We decided to say no to fast food on our sabbath days (Saturdays) and to say yes to feasts made from local ingredients, prepared with care, served with love and shared with friends. We also instituted screenless Saturdays, unplugging from the digital technology that isolates us from one another in favor of things we can do together in the physical world. We trade in the iPhones and Macs for the wePlay, weWalk and weRead. Over just twenty-four hours I feel myself decompress in remarkable ways. I write by hand again. I read a novel. I think about poetry. I talk less and I listen more. I feel less herky-jerky. When we have to go grocery shopping, we go together. When we have to do chores, we do them together. We go for a walk in town and run into friends. We fall asleep in the living room. We play board games after dinner. Things happen that I want to broadcast to the world on Facebook, Twitter and Instagram, but instead I keep them to myself, and by so doing catch a glimpse of what it meant that Mary, the mother of Jesus, "treasured up all these things and pondered them in her

heart" (Lk 2:19 NIV). I am reminded of something said by Judith
Shulevitz, a former *Slate* and *New York Times Book Review* col-
umnist, who wrote a book about her family's decision to start
keeping the sabbath:

> Our schedules are not the only thing the Sabbath would
> disrupt if it could. It would also rip a hole in all the shim-
> mering webs that give modern life its pleasing aura of weight-
> lessness—the networks that zap digitized voices and money
> and data from server to iPhone to GPS. In a world of brightness
> and portability and instantaneous intimacy, the Sabbath foists
> on the consciousness the blackness of night, the heaviness of
> objects, the miles that keep us apart.[14]

SABBATH IMAGINATION

Sabbath is a way of slowing down and becoming attentive to the
reconciling life of God in creation most immediately at hand, in all
its complexity and particularity. It affirms work by keeping work in
its proper bounds and reorienting it toward the glory of God. It is
also a way of reining in our consumptive desires and cultivating a
spirit of gratitude.

"He who has his mind on taking, no longer has it on what he has
taken," the French essayist Michel de Montaigne wrote in the six-
teenth century, though it's a pretty startling summation of the most
lamentable themes of US history. It's also a reminder that we have
to choose whether our approach to life will be primarily acquisitive
or inquisitive; it can't be both. Sabbath, celebrated as a corporate
spiritual discipline in our families and churches, can help us choose
the latter. We could also say that he who has his mind on taking no
longer has it on what he has been given. Inquisitiveness and gratitude: these are pillars of a life characterized by sabbath imagination
and sabbath wonder.

Sabbath imagination is developed in the context of community.

Sabbath was never intended to be merely a solo exercise that we observe—or ignore—on our own. From the beginning, sabbath provided the basic rhythm of public life for the Israelites, as seen in the calendar of festivals in Leviticus 23. God gave Israel the sabbath even before they were given the Ten Commandments. Sabbath trust is so integral to what it means to be part of God's chosen people that the Israelites were instructed to keep a jarful of manna in the ark of the covenant, an ever-present reminder of God's love and provision.

Sabbath gives us the spiritual space we need to recognize the gifts already in our communities and to give thanks to God for them. One of the reasons we're so keen on asset-based development (more on this in chapter nine) is that it starts with what is present, not what is absent. What is the "manna" for your church? And what is your jar? How does your church recognize, and then memorialize, God's abundant provision?

As we said in the previous chapter, good work is essential to the slow church vision. Sabbath, however, creates a space in our lives for contemplation, which is not merely reflecting on God and creation in abstract terms. Rather, contemplation should be framed by the particular situations of our lives as individuals and church communities. In addition to recognizing and memorializing God's abundant blessings in all their particularity, sabbath contemplation provides space for us to reflect on the work we are engaged in and how and why we do it. At my (Chris's) church, we have struggled to make sense of what the sabbath means for us as a community, but we have come to see our ongoing Sunday night conversation as an essential sabbath practice. This conversation is our way of creating space to reflect together on the scriptural story and the particularities of how we have been called to embody it together here in our neighborhood. Although it probably doesn't look like the solemn image of contemplation that most of us have in our heads, it is a contemplative sabbath practice for us and an important way that we make sense of the varieties of work that we have been called to do in our neighborhood.

Sabbath can also help us see seemingly intractable people in a whole new light. The same creator God who is gazing down at you with love and delight looks at your adversary the same way. Because it is the day we slow down enough that real proximity and conversation become possible, sabbath may be the perfect day to practice reconciliation. What if we—as individuals and as churches—opened up our tables (real and metaphorical) to folks who have annoyed us, undermined us, jockeyed for power at our expense or who have opposite worldviews?

Slow church communities are marked by their ability to rest and revel together, and to enjoy the time God has given them without anxiety. "When Christians practice the love of Christ, they enter into God's own life," Wirzba writes. "They begin to see others in the way God sees them, as worthy of care and in need of mercy and hope. *Christlike ministry forms the practical context in terms of which the world can appear as lovable and delightful.*"[15] He says later: "The meaning and goodness of others, that which makes them delightful, emerges in our loving interaction with them. We can't really take delight from a distance or in a condition of apathy or ignorance. . . . We don't really know others until we understand them in this light."[16] Sabbath is therefore a practice by which we are trained to be attentive to and to bear witness to God's loving work. Others are no longer simply a means to satisfy our individual desires (economic, sensual, etc.) but beloved creatures of God with whom we must be reconciled.

CONVERSATION STARTERS

1. What sorts of sabbath practices does your congregation have? What practices do you have of pausing and reflecting together on who God is and who you are and how you are being called to

follow in God's mission? If you don't have any shared sabbath practices, what small steps can you take together in this direction?

2. What is "enough"? What are the places in your life together, where you can transparently discuss your finances as individuals, as families and as a church and really strive to forge a common understanding in your congregation of what it means to have enough?

Third Course

8

Abundance

The Economy of Creation

[The myth of scarcity] ends in despair. It gives us a present tense of anxiety, fear, greed and brutality. It produces child and wife abuse, indifference to the poor, the buildup of armaments, divisions between people, and environmental racism. It tells us not to care about anyone but ourselves—and it is the prevailing creed of American society.

Walter Brueggemann

For the past several years, I (Chris) have kept a vegetable garden in our backyard. I'm not a very diligent gardener. I don't handle the heat well, and the busiest season in the garden is also the time of the year when I travel most. But one part of gardening I particularly enjoy, and have had some degree of success at, is seed saving. Seed saving is exactly what it sounds like. With the right varieties of plants, you can save seeds at the end of one season and use them for planting the next season. As I survey my garden this spring, for example, I see fifth-generation tomato plants and third-generation cucumbers and lettuce. Sure, there's a bit of knowledge required, and the seeds of some plants are more complicated to save than others. But the tools are ones we have on hand already—a knife, toilet paper (for blotting wet seeds like tomato seeds) and envelopes for storage. Overall, I am constantly amazed by how simple the process is. Even more than the simplicity, I am amazed by the sheer abundance present in the natural processes of plants. If I am careful and fortunate, the seeds of one modest-sized tomato can provide all the plants I need for my own garden next year and also enough for five or six additional people who are gardening on a similar scale. And that's just one tomato!

One tomato plant easily generates enough seed for thousands of new plants. Of course, we don't grow tomatoes primarily for their seeds; most of our tomatoes get eaten. Still, it's wondrous that God embeds in the very structure of an organism the provision for its own abundant flourishing. There are a host of factors that contribute to the successful germination and fruition of a seed—the kind of soil or other surface a seed falls on, the presence of animals who might eat the seed or seedlings, its proximity to other plants and so on—but God provides abundant resources for the plant to propagate on its own, which equals a staggering *super*abundance of resources if humans are engaged in cultivating and caring for the plant.

We see God's abundance not just in plants but throughout creation. Gerhard Lohfink (paraphrasing Joseph Ratzinger, who later became Pope Benedict XVI) puts it this way:

> Nature "luxuriates." What an opulence of flowers and butterflies alone! What a superfluity of seeds to produce a single living thing! What an expenditure of solar systems, Milky Ways, and spiral nebulae! An entire universe is squandered in order to produce more and more costly forms of life on a single planet and to prepare a place for the human spirit.[1]

UNMASKING THE MYTH OF SCARCITY

Despite the opulence of creation, the world's economic systems are built on a foundation of scarce resources. Scarcity is explicitly or implicitly given primacy of place in many definitions of economics as a social science. For example, one commonly accepted definition is from Lionel Robbins: "Economics is a science which studies human behavior as a relationship between ends and *scarce means* which have alternative uses."[2] The standard economic story is that if a resource is perceived to be scarce and the demand for it is high, then people will be willing to pay more for it and the price will go up. There are situations of real and apparent scarcity in the world; people die of hunger due to famines and complex socioeconomic systems that prevent the movement of sufficient food from places that have too much to famine areas. Greed functions to divert a staggering amount of resources from people most in need. Corruption at the national and local levels in Africa, Asia, South America and parts of Eastern Europe diverts the flow of resources and disproportionately affects the most vulnerable people in society. In 2005, the World Bank described a "Global Corruption Industry" and estimated the economic costs of bribery alone at 1 trillion dollars.[3]

Are there enough resources in creation for the sustenance of all life? This question is a complex one, and we can create vast systems that support a particular answer, but ultimately we can only answer in faith. Answering in the negative is a useful mythology for protecting the interests of wealthy nations and individuals. But the biblical narrative compels us to answer in the affirmative: God loves creation and has provided and will provide the sustenance that we need.

On one hand, we live in a culture that is driven by an economy rooted in the myth that there is not enough, but we also live within the biblical narrative that repeatedly emphasizes that God created the world and loves it immensely and will sustain it. We are a people being stretched to our very limits by this tension. We are too quick to submit to an economy that is sometimes in outright opposition to the deep magic that orders the universe. We'd like more of the stubborn dignity asserted by Wendell Berry in his essay "Discipline and Hope":

> If the Golden Rule were generally observed among us, the
> economy would not last a week. We have made our false
> economy a false god, and it has made blasphemy of the truth.
> So I have met the economy in the road, and am expected to
> yield it right of way. But I will not get over. My reason is that
> I am a man, and have a better right to the ground than the
> economy. The economy is no god for me, for I have had too
> close a look at its wheels. I have seen it at work in the strip
> mines and coal camps of Kentucky, and I know it has no
> moral limits.[4]

The economic machine has as its goal limitless growth, which
requires infinite fuel, separates the end from the means, and prizes
abstraction, quantity, efficiency and speed over mindfulness, quality,
discipline and relationships. (In the great recession of 2008 we've
caught a glimpse of what happens when the machine seizes up.)
Many Christians who oppose the teaching of evolution in school
accept unquestioningly an economic Darwinism that exalts competition, scoffs at cooperation, and leaves for dead the slow and
straggling wounded. "A better alternative is a better economy,"
writes Berry. "But we will not conceive the possibility of a better
economy, and therefore will not begin to change, until we quit deifying the present one."[5]

THE ECONOMY OF THE PRESENT AGE

Why does an economy rooted in the myth of scarcity seem so plausible to us? Why does it often appear that scarcity really does order
the world? The mythology of scarcity preys upon our fears, especially the fear that there will not be enough resources in the world
to provide for us, and thus that we might starve or otherwise suffer
from deprivation. In its pathological extreme, such fear leads to

hoarding resources. Reality television shows like *Hoarders* might provide some entertainment or even some relief that our tendencies toward hoarding aren't so bad, but they traffic on a basic fear that plagues us all that we will not have enough.

The myth of scarcity preys not only on our fears but also on our desires. In his book *Being Consumed: Economics and Christian Desire,* William Cavanaugh explores how our desires are shaped by the myth of scarcity and how we can submit our desires to be transformed by God and toward God. Cavanaugh writes that, according to the myth of scarcity, "there is never enough to go around. But it is not simply the hunger of those who lack sufficient food to keep their bodies in good health. Scarcity is the more general hunger of those who want more, without reference to what they already have."[6] Examining the work of St. Augustine on this subject, Cavanaugh concludes that desire is not the problem. "We desire because we live." Rather, the problem is that our desires are oriented toward things that will not satisfy. We desire things for their own sake. Only when our desires are oriented toward the Creator will we find fulfillment in the things of creation.

Our desires for more—more material things, as well as unhealthy relational desires—will never satisfy us, and yet we keep pursuing them, faster and faster we go. But God is calling us to step off this hamster wheel and trust in the abundance of divine provision. In the Sermon on the Mount, Jesus said:

> No one can serve two masters; for a slave will either hate the one and love the other, or be devoted to the one and despise the other. You cannot serve God and wealth.
>
> Therefore I tell you, do not worry about your life, what you will eat or what you will drink, or about your body, what you will wear. Is not life more than food, and the body more than clothing? (Mt 6:24-25)

In addition to speeding up the pace of our lives, the cycle of desire has the effect of blinding us toward the plight of others who face genuine deprivation. Rather than consuming our desires, our desires consume us, and we become oblivious to the struggles of others, even those closest to us. Cavanaugh makes the uncomfortable observation that under the myth of scarcity one can never have enough, and charitable giving "is relegated to the private realm of preference, not justice. One can always send a check to help feed the hungry, but one's charitable preferences will always be in competition with one's own endless desires."[7] Thus, the myth of scarcity fuels the inherent self-centeredness of capitalism. In this regard, Cavanaugh points to Adam Smith's *Theory of Moral Sentiments*:

> Men, though not naturally sympathetic, feel so little for one another, with whom they have no particular connection, in comparison of what they feel for themselves; the misery of one, who is merely their fellow-creature, is of so little importance to them in comparison even of a small conveniency of their own.[8]

CHURCHES IN THE ECONOMY OF SCARCITY

Similarly, the economy of the present age, rooted in scarcity, all too often holds our churches in a death grip: in the interest of survival we cling desperately to resources, sharing them sparingly, if at all, with others in need. Scarcity impedes our imaginations, compelling us to conclude, "We could never do that." Although churches can exist without paid staff or buildings—and indeed many churches throughout history have—some churches, faced with ever-tightening budgets, have shut their doors. Similarly, a recent Barna report notes that churches respond to diminished budgets by (1) reducing spending, (2) cutting staffing or missions, and/or (3) reducing facility budgets.[9] All of these sorts of actions are reasonable, but it's striking that they all focus on the expenditure side of the ledger and not the income side.

Luther Snow tells a compelling story of a suburban congregation that increased its income by 50 percent one year by revitalizing its stewardship committee. This committee had been all but dead; no one would volunteer for it, but as the congregation began to map out the assets that they had available to them, a new, re-energized committee emerged. Leveraging their assets included growing and selling vegetables on their land and making space in their building available for neighborhood groups. One leader of this church said:

> There's so much going on, and we keep finding new connections to make things happen. Everybody is helping each other out or piggybacking one thing with another. We have worked together on lots of little fundraisers to fill in the gaps. One day we had a gathering of a bunch of the leaders to share our news and plans and ideas. Somebody said we should meet regularly. Somebody else said, "Right, and we should cooperate on a larger fundraising campaign to save time."

The group assembled for this meeting became the church's new and re-energized stewardship committee.[10] Scarcity often has the effect of blinding our churches to the abundant resources that God has provided for our life together. To make the leap from an economy of scarcity to an economy of abundance, we need to begin by immersing ourselves in the biblical story and allowing God to transform our minds and imaginations.

SCARCITY AND ABUNDANCE IN THE EXODUS STORY

"The myth of scarcity," as Walter Brueggemann has named it, is useful for subjugating peoples, and for helping the rich stay rich and the powerful stay in power. This mythology is rooted in the fear of losing wealth, power and privilege, which has led to gruesome results throughout human history. Brueggemann uses the biblical story of Pharaoh and the Israelites to illustrate:

Because Pharaoh . . . is afraid that there aren't enough good things to go around, he must try to have them all. Because he is fearful, he is ruthless. Pharaoh hires Joseph to manage the monopoly. When crops fail and the peasants run out of food, they come to Joseph. And on behalf of Pharaoh, Joseph says, "What's your collateral?" They give you their land for food, and then, the next year, they give up their cattle. By the third year of the famine, they have no collateral but themselves. And that's how the children of Israel become slaves—through an economic transaction.[11]

In time, Pharaoh owns all of the Israelites' land, except the land belonging to the priests. He leaves the priests' land alone because their blessing is a key element of the propaganda that keeps the mythology of scarcity alive. Though the Israelites are slaves, the abundance of God's creation is still at work in their midst. The Israelites keep having children, so many children, in fact, that the fast-growing Israelite population begins to be perceived as a threat. Pharaoh issues an edict that all Hebrew babies should be killed. The Hebrew midwives creatively resist this cruel decree, and some babies continue to survive, including Moses, who will mature to be Israel's leader.

A good chunk of the biblical story of Exodus is, in essence, the story of Pharaoh's fearful brutality against the Israelites. It's only after repeatedly failing to subdue the Israelites that Pharaoh gives up in exasperation. He summons Moses and Aaron and tells them to take their people and get out of Egypt. But before they leave, Pharaoh asks them to bless him. Brueggemann offers a poignant interpretation of this surprising request:

> [The] great king of Egypt, who presides over a monopoly of the region's resources, asks Moses and Aaron to bless him. The powers of scarcity admit to this little community of abundance "It is clear that you are the wave of the future. So before you leave,

lay your powerful hands upon us and give us energy." The text shows that the power of the future is not in the hands of those who believe in scarcity and monopolize the world's resources; it is in the hand of those who trust God's abundance.[12]

As the Israelites wander in the wilderness, they waver in their faith. They grumble against Moses and Aaron. They wonder if life under the tyranny of scarcity was better than this new life in the desert. It's at this point in the biblical narrative that we encounter one of the most unexpected lines in all of Scripture: "Then the Lord said to Moses, 'I am going to rain bread from heaven for you" (Ex 16:4). Five days a week the Israelites gather a day's portion of bread. The name the Israelites give the bread (manna, from the Hebrew words meaning "What is it?") reflects their perplexity about this new kind of bread they can't create or control. At first, they are content with the manna, which was like coriander seed and tasted like wafers made with honey. But eventually some people try to hoard it. So powerful was the myth of scarcity in Egypt that it was difficult for their imaginations to be transformed, even after they had been set free.

God instructs the Israelites not to gather manna on the sabbath (the seventh day) but instead to gather two portions of bread on the sixth day. Sabbath observance is a hedge against the tyranny of the myth of scarcity. "People who think their lives consist of struggling to get more and more," says Brueggemann, "can never slow down because they won't ever have enough."[13] Resting on the sabbath, the Israelites learn to trust in God's abundant provision.

The book of Exodus says the people of Israel ate manna for forty years, until they came to a habitable land. God's provision of manna ended, though God's economy of superabundance did not; the Israelites were in a land where they had the means to grow their own food, the Promised Land, described as a land flowing with milk and honey.

A LITANY OF GOD'S ABUNDANT PROVISION

Scarcity is a pretender to the throne. The law of God's household is life, not death; windfall, not shortfall; provision, not lack; and it is characterized by the radical immanence of God in the Spirit. God's economy is preeminent over markets free or otherwise. God's economy is the standard by which all historical economies will be judged. From the very outset, Scripture teaches us that the economy of God's kingdom is one of vast abundance, a word that derives from the Latin for "overflowing." Walter Brueggemann describes the creation story as a "liturgy of abundance." Not only does God call the creation good—with the implication that it is lacking in nothing—it is also created with the capacity for proliferation. And proliferate it does, with God's blessing to "be fruitful and multiply" (Gen 1:11-12, 22, 28).

The Psalms are full of the praises of God's abundance. Psalm 104 is a powerful hymn to the abundance of God, and as Brueggemann has noted, it is a commentary on Genesis 1. God creates the waters and orchestrates their movements so that the thirst of all creation is filled. All the beasts of the field, all the birds of the air, everyone— "the earth is satisfied with the fruit of [God's] work" (Ps 104:13). The plants provide abundantly for the sustenance and shelter of all God's creatures: food from the earth, wine that gladdens the heart of men, oil to make his face shine, trees to provide homes for birds and other creatures (Ps 104:14-17). The earth and sea teem with life (Ps 104:24-25). And we are all sustained by God, as we see in Genesis 1:

> So God created humankind in his image,
>   in the image of God he created them;
>   male and female he created them.
>
> God blessed them, and God said to them, "Be fruitful and multiply, and fill the earth and subdue it; and have dominion over the fish of the sea and over the birds of the air and over

every living thing that moves upon the earth." God said, "See, I have given you every plant yielding seed that is upon the face of all the earth, and every tree with seed in its fruit; you shall have them for food. And to every beast of the earth, and to every bird of the air, and to everything that creeps on the earth, everything that has the breath of life, I have given every green plant for food." And it was so. (Gen 1:27-30)

Jesus' words "I am the bread of life" (Jn 6:35) seem to echo verses 27-28 of Psalm 104: "[All the creatures] look to you to give them their food in due season; when you give to them, they gather it up; when you open your hand, they are filled with good things." When we reject God and cause God to go into hiding (so to speak), the psalmist says that we become dismayed (Ps 104:29). In our terror we cling doggedly to the world's resources.

One of our favorite stories of God's abundance in the New Testament is the one often called the feeding of the five thousand (Mk 6:30-44). In the story, Jesus and his disciples get into a boat to go to a desolate place where they can rest and eat. But they are recognized from a distance, and thousands of people from neighboring towns gather on the shore to meet them. When Jesus sees the great crowd, "he had compassion on them, because they were like sheep without a shepherd" (Mk 6:34).

Jesus teaches the crowd many things. When it starts to get late, the disciples urge Jesus to send the crowd into the countryside and neighboring villages to buy food. Though the disciples seem to have good intentions, they engage the problem through the lens of the myth of scarcity. The disciples don't have enough food to feed everyone, so the people should be sent away to fend for themselves. By the wisdom of the world, the disciples' plan ("Let's all go dutch") is a reasonable one. But Jesus dismisses this approach with the astonishing command, "You give them something to eat" (v. 37).

The disciples do the math, calculating how much it will cost to

feed a crowd this size. "Should we go and buy two hundred denarii worth of bread?" they ask. (Two hundred denarii is the
equivalent of two hundred days' wages for a laborer.) This is obviously more money than the disciples have, so their question has
the tone of, "And where are we going to get that kind of money?"
But Jesus goes even further. He knows that the disciples' cost es-
timate allows only for the minimum sustenance, so he rejects this
idea as well. Lohfink notes:

> The reign of God is far more than that! In it not only will need
> be satisfied; its essence is superabundance. In the reign of God
> the divine fullness will shine forth. But above all: an act of
> well-organized aid such as the disciples suggest would not
> really change the world. Society would remain what it is. It
> would constantly produce new structures of misery and the
> disciples would have to run panting back and forth non-stop
> to organize help for the hungry without ever putting an end
> to suffering.[14]

Jesus asks the disciples to do an inventory of the available food,
and they come up with five loaves of bread and two fish. Most of
us are familiar with the end of the story: everyone eats their fill, and
twelve baskets of leftovers are collected at the end. But we often
overlook two interesting aspects of the story. The first is that before
Jesus blesses the food and breaks the bread, he instructs his disciples to organize the crowd into groups of hundreds and fifties.
This is an order reminiscent of Moses' organization of the Israelites
in Exodus 18:25. Lohfink suggests that Jesus arranged the people
into small clusters so they could ensure that everyone in their
groups would be fed. This story is miraculous on many levels, one
of which is that the gathered multitude didn't act according to the
myth of scarcity, but generously shared their food with their groups.
This is, in Lohfink's words, "a miracle drawn from what is already
present," the superabundant providence of God.

The second often overlooked aspect is that we have misnamed the story. For one thing, "five thousand" refers to the thousands of men who were there but not the women and children. Also, as Lohfink has pointed out, what unfolded on the shore in Galilee was not a mere "feeding" but an extraordinary feast. We see this in Jesus' instruction that the crowd should recline (Mk 6:39). In the ancient world, everyday meals were eaten while sitting, but special, festive banquets were enjoyed in a reclining posture. Furthermore, the fact that twelve baskets of food were collected after everyone had eaten their fill gives us a sense of how bountiful the meal was. Lohfink argues that this banquet was a sign to the early church that the abundant kingdom of God had broken into the world:

> Jesus proclaims that the future has arrived. It is present. The joy of the end of time has already begun. God's festal banquet with God's people, Israel, which is to expand into a feast for all nations, is beginning. Jesus is so certain that the reign of God is now a reality, a richly abundant meal, that he calls his poor, hungry hearers, blessed: "Blessed are you who are hungry now, for you will be filled" (Luke 6:21). One may promise the hungry that they will be filled if one expects the promise to be fulfilled not after death and not in some uncertain future, but in a future that is already beginning.[15]

BEARING WITNESS TO THE ABUNDANCE OF GOD'S KINGDOM

How do slow churches bear witness to the abundant economy of God's kingdom in today's world? The essential practices of this new economy are first gratitude, then generosity and hospitality. We'll explore these practices in subsequent chapters. But before we do so, let's look briefly at the context in which they unfold, since we are presumably gathered—like the crowd in the above Gospel story— into eucharistic dining communities we call churches.

Perhaps the most powerful biblical story of a community bearing

witness to the abundant economy of God's kingdom is the story of
the people who gathered in Jerusalem after Pentecost. We read in
Acts 4:

> Now the whole group of those who believed were of one heart
> and soul, and no one claimed private ownership of any pos-
> sessions, but everything they owned was held in common.
> With great power the apostles gave their testimony to the
> resurrection of the Lord Jesus, and great grace was upon them
> all. There was not a needy person among them, for as many
> as owned lands or houses sold them and brought the proceeds
> of what was sold. They laid it at the apostles' feet, and it was
> distributed to each as any had need. There was a Levite, a
> native of Cyprus, Joseph, to whom the apostles gave the name
> Barnabas (which means "son of encouragement"). He sold a
> field that belonged to him, then brought the money, and laid
> it at the apostles' feet. (vv. 32-27)

These early Christians weren't driven to hoard by greed or fear.
When needs or opportunities arose, the people who had resources
stepped up and made them available. Poverty had been abolished
among the group. This story has captured the economic imaginations of various Christian groups throughout the last two millennia
(for example, certain monastic and Anabaptist communities), but
it largely fails to do so among Western churches today.

Embodying the abundance of God's kingdom in our local
ekklesia is not only incredibly countercultural, it is also strikingly
timely. Economic crises reveal how deeply embedded the mythology of scarcity is in our culture. Talk of the economy has dominated our news and politics since the financial collapse in 2008.
When is the housing market going to rebound? How many millions of lost jobs aren't going to come back? Are we headed for a
double-dip recession or, worse, another great depression? These
and other questions race through our minds. But the mythology

of scarcity doesn't just plague us as individuals; it also plagues our churches. Many churches, particularly urban ones, have already folded or soon will.[16] Sustaining smaller churches with shrinking congregations is a major challenge for most mainline denominations. Closing a church or merging congregations aren't necessarily bad things, if these moves are done with careful attentiveness to the parishioners and the neighborhoods these churches serve. But we suspect that if we took God's abundance seriously, most churches could be sustainable.

Imagination is key. It's a failure of imagination when we get locked into the scarcity mentality and can't see the resources God has provided for us. Perhaps many smaller churches aren't financially sustainable because they are reliant solely on the offering plate. However, most of the big-budget items small churches deem to be necessities—especially staff and facilities—are not actually essential. Many churches throughout history have thrived without paid staff and dedicated buildings. Cutting staff shouldn't be our first course of action, as it may not be a loving response toward the people involved. However, if staff leave, there should be serious conversation about if and how they should be replaced. Choosing not to fill an open staff position is a great opportunity to encourage non-staffers to step up and become more deeply involved in the life and the work of the church. Englewood Christian Church (Chris's church) was once a very large church with a large pastoral staff, but as the size of the congregation shrank, more and more staff were laid off. With fewer pastors, the congregation began to take on much of the work that the staff had historically done: planning music or children's activities, managing the budget, counseling struggling neighbors, visiting the sick and the elderly. Today, Englewood only has one pastor on staff, and he is very engaged with community development and daycare work and spends only part of his time doing traditional pastoral work. This gradual shift in how the work of the church gets done has led our congregation as a whole to a deeper sense of ownership and commitment to the work that we have been called to as a church community.

Similarly, we need to think creatively about how our church facilities are owned, used and maintained. Again, a church building isn't a necessity. There are many benefits of meeting in homes, as many of the early Christians did. Churches that do have dedicated buildings should look to see if those facilities can be sold, rented or used more carefully throughout the week to generate economic activity. From renting meeting space or office space to starting micro-businesses, there is a host of possibilities. There are also many ways that a church building can be maintained. One church I (Chris) used to be a part of saved money on janitorial costs by creating a schedule in which all of the small groups in the congregation would each clean the building on a rotation once every couple of months. This endeavor was well organized; there was a checklist of cleaning tasks that needed to be done every week, and with ten to twenty people pitching in together, cleaning the church building from top to bottom went quickly and enjoyably. Some small groups reported that cleaning the church building was a fun interruption of their regular meetings for Bible study and conversation; they often would highlight the evening by going out to eat together.

THINKING OUTSIDE THE OFFERING PLATE

When it comes to generating income, churches need to think outside the offering plate. Do we, like the early Christians in Jerusalem, believe our resources are held in common? Do we make them available when needs and opportunities arise? Churches can leverage the resources they already have to generate continuing income—from the familiar (preschools, bookstores, coffee shops) to the peculiar (farming, coffee roasting, apartment rental). Many churches are finding creative ways to use the skills of their members and the resources of their neighborhoods to generate income.

If your church's staff budget is in a pinch, maybe you can start a business that would utilize the skills of one or more staff members and help subsidize the costs of keeping them on staff. This new enterprise should be more than just a way to make money; it should promote the flourishing of the neighborhood in some way: creating jobs, connecting neighbors, and providing needed goods and services. For instance, there is a Christian and Missionary Alliance congregation in central Indiana that had a pastor for many years who had a passion for coffee. Having started at the church in a lean period in its history, the pastor supplemented his income by working part time in the coffee trade, and he also worked with the church to start a number of coffee-related businesses—roasting coffee, selling equipment and consulting with coffeehouses. These businesses thrived over time and eventually provided a financial base for the church to launch a ministry internship for young adults, where interns worked with the coffee businesses part time and also studied Scripture and got experience in pastoral ministry. In conjunction with their coffee business, the church often hosted coffeehouse concerts and freely served their amazing coffee at their services, all of which contributed to a warm and hospitable environment that helped to build up the church.

North United Methodist Church in Indianapolis has coordinated a weekly farmers' market on their property for over ten years. This market, which is run completely by volunteers, not only gives a boost to the local economy by providing a space where farmers and artisans can sell their locally produced goods, but it also has been marked by a keen focus on getting good and delicious produce into the hands of those who might not otherwise be able to afford it. Located in close proximity to some of the city's most economically challenged neighborhoods, the church's farmers' market was one of the first in the city to accept government-subsidized vouchers for low-income families. However, in 2011, the church took a bold step above and beyond the government assistance by matching the government subsidy dollar for dollar with their own funds.

Though we have mentioned only a few possibilities in the preceding paragraphs—and those only quickly—we hope that it has become clear that God has provided us with abundant resources. The pressing questions are these: Are we willing to creatively and faithfully plug in to the abundant economy of God? Will we submit the resources we have been given (as individuals and as church families) to the work of God's kingdom? Are we being attentive to the gifts God has given us, not only in our congregations but also in our neighborhoods?

From hosting farmers' markets to sharing each other's financial burdens to leasing out space in our church buildings, there are many ways to nurture the redemptive work already under way among our neighbors. It is crucial, however, that we remain attentive to the scale on which we do the work that we do. The work we undertake should reflect the resources we are able to invest in it. We often fall into the trap of thinking that if we can't do something in a big way, it shouldn't be done at all. Though we should do our work well, our end is not to bring glory to ourselves with large and well-received ventures, but to bear witness to the in-breaking of God's kingdom, the peculiar and redemptive way of Jesus.

"God's work done in God's way," the great missionary Hudson Taylor famously said, "will never lack God's supply." As the witness of the early church reminds us, it is possible for God's people to incarnate an alternative to the economics of scarcity. As Michael Frost, Alan Hirsch and others have convincingly demonstrated, the Christendom approach to church, which imposes order from the top down, is of waning effectiveness. We can't impose a new economic order on society. Rather, the economy of abundance will arise from the grassroots of our local congregations as we model new ways of sharing life together. As we seek to thrive in deeper and more creative ways on a local and sustainable scale, we will get a taste of God's superabundance. And as we grow in faithful witness to God's economy, our economic relations will extend beyond our care for one another in our local congregations. In one of his sabbath poems, Wendell Berry says of hope:

> It lights invariably the need for care
> toward other people, other creatures, in other places
> as you would ask them for care toward your place and you.[17]

In the following chapters, we will explore three practices of the church that will form us more deeply into the superabundant economy that God has intended for creation. Specifically, we will first examine the practice of gratitude, our response to God's superabundant provision. We also will explore how that gratitude gets embodied in practices of generosity and hospitality. We follow God's lead when we abundantly and generously share God's gifts with others in our congregations, our neighborhoods and around the globe.

CONVERSATION STARTERS

1. What are some ways that God has provided abundantly for the flourishing of your church community? Describe and reflect on the specifics of God's provision in these situations.

2. What resources does your church have in the gifts and skills of your members or in your land and buildings that could be leveraged to benefit the well-being of your congregation or your neighbors? Pay particular attention to the gifts of those that we tend to marginalize: the young (children and youth) and the old, those with physical or emotional challenges, and so on.

3. Are there ways in which you as a church are hoarding resources and withholding them from members or neighbors who might richly benefit from access to them?

9

Gratitude

Receiving the Good Gifts of God

Get up in the morning and look at the
world in a way that takes nothing for granted.
Everything is phenomenal; everything is incredible; never
treat life casually. To be spiritual is to be amazed.

Abraham Heschel, *Between God and Man*

In chapter eight, we talked about the abundance of God's household, an abundance that flows from the fullness of a God who is "at hand . . . and not a God far away." "'Do I not fill heaven and earth?' declares the Lord" (Jer 23:23-24 ESV). The apostle Paul was speaking of this radically abundant and yet radically immanent God when he prayed that the church in Ephesus, "being rooted and grounded in love," might have "the power to comprehend, with all the saints, what is the breadth and length and height and depth, and to know the love of Christ that surpasses knowledge, so that you may be filled with all the fullness of God" (Eph 3:17-19).

In chapter ten, we will look at hospitality and generosity, two ways slow churches live into an abundant economy of God that seems wholly incompatible with market systems that make a virtue of selfishness. Open-handed generosity and caring for the poor and marginalized as if we were caring for Jesus himself are extensions of our worship. They are also acts of obedience that can plant the seeds of God's love in hearts and transform our houses, churches and neighborhoods into outposts of peace and reconciliation.

The topic of this chapter is gratitude, which is a vital bridge between abundance and generosity. As a spiritual discipline—one that requires time and intentionality, both on our own and in community—gratitude is how we practice recognizing the abundant gifts God has given us. It's how we praise God for those gifts. And it is the energy that compels us to want to share those gifts. As the writer of Hebrews put it, "Through [Jesus], then, let us continually offer a sacrifice of praise to God, that is, the fruit of lips that confess his name. Do not neglect to do good and to share what you have, for such sacrifices are pleasing to God" (13:15-16).

THE GENEROSITY OF THE SOCIAL GOD

Gratitude is one of the most important themes in Scripture. As we live into Scripture we soon realize that God is a *giver*. God "made the world and everything in it," and "gives to all mortals life and breath and all things" (Acts 17:24-25). God gives strength (Ps 68:35; Phil 4:13), gives us the sun (Jer 31:35) and the rain (Zech 10:1), and gives the spirit of wisdom and revelation (Eph 1:17). God gives grace to the humble (Jas 4:6). God gives peace and rest (Is 14:3; Num 6:26). God comforts those who mourn, gives them beauty for ashes, the oil of joy for mourning and the garment of praise for a heavy spirit (Is 61:2-3).

The whole foundation of the universe rests on this central attribute of God's character: God gives because it is God's nature to give. This is why many theologians have described the gifting God as a kind of fountain. John Calvin called God the "fountain of goodness and mercy," and Martin Luther called God "an eternal fountain overflowing with sheer goodness." St. Bonaventure described God as *fontalis plenitude,* the "fountain-fullness." As one eighteenth-century hymn says:

> Come, Thou Fount of every blessing,
> Tune my heart to sing Thy grace;
> Streams of mercy, never ceasing,
> Call for songs of loudest praise.

We read throughout the New Testament about the generous love the three members of the Trinity have for each other. For example, we read that God the Father delights in the Son (Mt 3:17; 17:5) and gives all things to the Son (Jn 3:35). But perhaps this perfect fellowship is nowhere more evident than in John 14–17, which recounts a conversation Jesus has with his disciples not long before his death, a passage so exhilarating that when it's read in one sitting it can leave you breathless and whirling and maybe even laughing. There we read that the Father gives to the Son, the Son gives to the Father, and the Son asks the Father to give the Holy Spirit. Royce G. Gruenler captures the divine family dynamic well when he writes about the "generosity of the social God": "The manner of Jesus' speech indicates his conviction that the persons of the divine Community inwardly enjoy one another's love, hospitality, generosity, and interpersonal communion, so much that they are one God, and being one God, express such love to one another."[1]

What's also extraordinary about the passage in John is that it describes how the perfect community of the Father, Son and Holy Spirit has been expanded to embrace humanity. "I am in my Father, and you in me, and I in you," Jesus says (14:20). So the Father glorifies the Son, the Son glorifies the Father and the Holy Spirit glorifies the Son. But the Son also glorifies his followers, who in turn glorify the Father before the watching world!

"Abide in me as I abide in you," Jesus says to his friends, offering them divine hospitality. (These are two of the eleven times the word "abide" will appear over a span of seven verses.) "Just as the branch cannot bear fruit by itself unless it abides in the vine, neither can you unless you abide in me. I am the vine, you are the branches. Those who abide in me and I in them bear much fruit, because apart from me you can do nothing" (Jn 15:4-5). The key to abiding is thankfulness. In gratitude we remain on the vine, receive our sustenance and are fruitful.

Jesus exhorts his followers to love each other, and he prays that they would have a oneness modeled on the generous, delighting and self-giving unity of the Father, Son and Spirit. He prays for the church:

> As you, Father, are in me and I am in you, may they also be in us, so that the world may believe that you have sent me. The glory that you have given me I have given them, so that they may be one, as we are one, I in them and you in me, that they may become completely one, so that the world may know that you have sent me and have loved them even as you have loved me. (Jn 17:21-23)

Jesus also promises continued provision, even after he has returned to the Father. "Until now you have not asked for anything in my name. Ask and you will receive," he says, "so that your joy may be complete" (Jn 16:24).

A THANKFUL PEOPLE

Since the earliest days of Abraham, Isaac and Jacob, gratitude has been the defining characteristic of how the people of God abide in the loving community of the Trinity. God provides, and we, at our very best, respond with praise and thanksgiving. Jacob expresses his gratitude for God's protection and provision as he flees his brother Esau by erecting a pillar as a memorial that he names Beth-el (the house of God) and by offering sacrifices there. The Torah, the law that ordered and gave shape to the Israelite people, instructed them to make offerings of thanksgiving (Lev 7:11-34), which Leviticus also refers to as peace offerings—or in some

English translations, fellowship offerings—a reminder of the community of *shalom* into which God has called us. In her excellent
book *Living into Community,* Christine Pohl observes that the ancient Israelites cultivated gratitude in their life and worship by
"speaking of God's deeds among the people, and remembering and
telling of God's blessing, wonderful works and faithfulness."[2] The
Psalms, the book of common prayer for the ancient Israelites, are
full of praise and thanksgiving for God's abundant provision. "Sing
praises to the LORD, O you his faithful ones, and give thanks to his
holy name" (Ps 30:4). "Then I will thank you in the great congregation; in the mighty throng I will praise you" (Ps 35:18). "In God
we have boasted continually, and we will give thanks to your name
forever" (Ps 44:8).

The New Testament churches were similarly marked by their
gratitude. Thanksgiving is a recurring theme in the writings of the
apostle Paul. More than three-quarters of the uses of *eucharisteo*
(thanksgiving) and *charis* (grace) in the New Testament occur in
Paul's writings. And, according to some scholars, Paul mentions
thanksgiving more frequently per page than any other Hellenistic
writer of his time.[3] In 1 Thessalonians, for example, Paul says, "Be
at peace among yourselves. And we urge you, beloved, to admonish the idlers, encourage the fainthearted, help the weak, be
patient with all of them. See that none of you repays evil for evil,
but always seek to do good to one another and to all. Rejoice
always, pray without ceasing, give thanks in all circumstances; for
this is the will of God in Christ Jesus for you" (5:13-18). There are
rows of books in Christian bookstores on finding the perfect center
of God's will for your life. But here it is, plain as can be: to pray
and to give thanks.

In another letter, Paul urges the Christians in Colossae to "let the
word of Christ dwell in you richly; teach and admonish one another
in all wisdom; and with gratitude in your hearts sing psalms, hymns,
and spiritual songs to God. And whatever you do, in word or deed,

do everything in the name of the Lord Jesus, giving thanks to God the Father through him" (Col 3:16-17).

THE CYCLE OF FORGETFULNESS AND RESTORATION

If the essence of God is to give, the essence of humanity is thankfulness.[4] But in a fallen world it hasn't always worked out that way. The story of Scripture is the gathering of a people that will make God's goodness known to the world. But time and again, as we've seen, humans have been ungrateful. In fact, a case can be made that ingratitude was the original sin in the garden. Certainly ingratitude is at the root of many other sins, including envy, covetousness, lust and even idolatry, for in the Old Testament, forgetting God was tantamount to idolatry (2 Kings 17:38; Jer 13:25; 18:15). Christine Pohl writes: "In Scripture, remembering falsely or forgetting entirely is often associated with an absence of gratitude. One of the saddest judgments passed on people in Scripture is that they didn't remember God's steadfast love."[5]

And yet even in the midst of this forgetfulness, God draws near. In the book of Hosea, Israel is compared to an adulterous wife, but God declares that he is going to allure her, lead her into the wilderness and speak tenderly to her, and restore her to perfect relationship (Hos 2:14). In the book of Nehemiah, Ezra stands up before the people of Israel to make a national confession. He recalls the ancestors who refused to obey God's commandments and "were not mindful of the wonders that you performed among them." And yet, Ezra says, "you are a God ready to forgive, gracious and merciful, slow to anger and abounding in steadfast love" (Neh 9:17).

The cycle of forgetfulness, judgment and restoration continued throughout the ages of the prophets, priests and kings. It culminated in the life, death and resurrection of Jesus—the one Prophet, Priest and King. Jesus' crucifixion was the ultimate gift, and the Eucharist (from a Greek word meaning "thanksgiving") is primarily an act of grateful remembering. As we will see, gratitude and ingratitude are at the heart of justice and injustice. Thus, it may be significant that the apostle Paul warns the Corinthians to learn from Israel's history of ingratitude (1 Cor 10:1-6), and then one chapter later rebukes them for celebrating the Eucharist in ways that cause disunity and reinforce old social and economic divisions (11:17-34).

FROM DISSATISFACTION TO SATISFACTION

We live in a consumerist culture that encourages forgetfulness. Dissatisfaction is at the very root of our modern economy. We're so immersed in the consumer culture that it's easy to assume things have always been this way. But that isn't the case. Back in 2002, the BBC produced a four-part documentary called *The Century of Self*, which detailed how, over the last ninety years, the principles of Freudian psychology have been used by corporations and politicians to subtly control a restive population. After World War I, corporations that had grown rich and powerful churning out war materiel and other mass-produced goods grew concerned about overproduction, concerned that the American people would be satisfied with what they already had. If people stopped buying things, the factories would go quiet and the boom years would be over. Paul Mazur, a prominent banker who joined Lehman Brothers in 1927, articulated the corporate response this way: "We must shift America from a needs to a desires culture. People must be trained to desire, to want new things, even before the old have been entirely consumed. Man's desires must overshadow his needs."

For help, corporations turned to Edward Bernays, a nephew of Sigmund Freud. Bernays had been a member of the Committee on Public Information, a government agency created by Woodrow Wilson to help convince Americans that the United States should join the war in Europe. When Bernays realized at the conclusion of the war how successful he had been in selling the image of Wilson as a liberator making the world safe for democracy, he wondered if he could use the same tactics in peacetime. He set up an office in the heart of Manhattan and began offering his services to big business and Republican politicians. Because the word *propaganda* had developed negative connotations, he called his work "public relations."

Freud believed that human behavior is driven more by irrational forces and instinct than it is by rational intellect. Bernays used this as his starting point to tap into and manipulate the unconscious desires of the crowd. He manufactured discontent to sell people things they didn't really need, and he connected the consumption of certain products to a search for the self. For example, Bernays convinced car companies they could sell their cars as symbols of male sexuality. On behalf of the American Tobacco Board, Bernays helped break the taboo against women smoking cigarettes. To do this, he staged a rally of wealthy debutantes smoking cigarettes while marching in New York's annual Easter parade. He called the cigarettes "torches of freedom," and they became icons of independent thinking.

Bernays also used the techniques of public relations to advance his politics. (He coined the phrase "engineered consent.") During the Eisenhower administration, he exploited American fear of Soviet expansion to sell a US-backed coup in Guatemala. A quarter century earlier, he had vigorously promoted Hebert Hoover's vision of American progress. Hoover reciprocated, telling a group of advertisers and public relations men after his 1928 election, "You have taken over the job of creating desire and have transformed people into constantly moving happiness machines, machines which have become the key to economic progress."[6]

Bernays, whom *Life* magazine later named one of the most influential Americans of the twentieth century, was an important part—though only a part, of course—in shaping the culture of the all-consuming self. It is a culture driven by a perpetual dissatisfaction machine that inundates us with the message that our lives won't be complete until we have the shiniest toy, the latest gadget, the most exclusive memberships, a younger wife, smoother skin, bouncier

hair, the right brands, a nicer car and a bigger house. We're surrounded by advertising and other media that tells us from an early
age that it is possible to buy happiness . . . at least until the next
must-have item comes around.

This dissatisfaction is at the root of a staggering amount of injustice. The idea that somehow we don't have access to everything
we need or deserve can lead to distrust, broken relationships,
ruthless competition, war, hunger, poverty, gross economic inequality and the wanton destruction of the natural world. Dissatisfaction is also connected to some of the more subtle forces, like
hypermobility, that undermine our neighborhoods, communities
and churches. On the other hand, says Mary Jo Leddy, a Canadian
theologian and social activist, the "choice to affirm that *there is
enough for all* is the beginning of social community, peace, and
justice. The option to assume that *there is enough* frees the imagination to think of new political and economic possibilities."[7]

Gratitude is perhaps the most important way we practice recognizing the enough all around us. If lack is the root of injustice, then
gratitude is the root of justice. How can we hoard what isn't ours?
How can Americans claim special privilege when God gives so indis-
criminately? And if everything we have is a gift from God, how can
we not share those gifts, even with our enemies (Mt 5:43-45, 48)?

Gratitude can help our faith communities move from dissatisfaction, fear and narcissism to satisfaction, trust and a deeper appre-
ciation of the interconnectedness of all things. It frees us up to live
in the present and to accept each moment and every circumstance as
a gift. "In gratitude," writes Leddy, "the vicious cycle of dissatisfaction with life is broken and we begin anew in the recognition of
what we have rather than in the awareness of who we aren't."[8]

CULTIVATING A GIFTS PERSPECTIVE

Gratitude requires practice, both in our personal lives and in the
shared life of our church communities; we must cultivate it in all

facets of our lives. Maybe you start by making a personal commitment to begin and end each day with words of praise. Or resolve to be more vigilant in saying thank you to people in your community who have been a blessing. Maybe you institute a new family tradition, as John and his family did, to start each meal by recounting three specific things you are grateful for in that moment. Or maybe some folks in your house church or Sunday school class decide to start keeping and sharing entries from a gratitude journal. While gratitude will never be so automatic that we can stop being intentional about it, it won't take long before we start seeing the world with new eyes. All around us are traces of God's blessings. Gratitude reveals just how porous the line is between the material and the spiritual.[9]

Cultivating a gifts perspective in our slow church communities makes us alive to, receptive of and thankful for God's abundant provision, which is daily discovered in even the humblest acts of grace. "Be thankful for the smallest blessing, and you will deserve to receive greater," Thomas à Kempis wrote in his fifteenth-century devotional classic, *The Imitation of Christ.* "Value the least gifts no less than the greatest, and simple graces as especial favors. If you remember the dignity of the Giver, no gift will seem small or mean, for nothing can be valueless that is given by the most high God."[10]

Giving thanks for a small gift can be the catalyst God uses to do something even more dramatic. There's an example of this in the story of the feeding of the four thousand in Mark 8. Not long after he fed a crowd of five thousand with only five loaves of bread and two fish, Jesus found himself surrounded by another huge crowd. They had been following him for three days but had nothing to eat. Jesus pressed his disciples to do something. But the disciples responded by saying, "How can one feed these people with bread here in the desert?"

The disciples' focus was on what they *lacked.* Jesus was focused on what they *had.* He took an inventory of the food at hand, which

amounted to seven loaves of bread, and then ordered the crowd to
sit down. He gave thanks for the bread and told his disciples to
distribute it. Then someone found a few small fish. After blessing
the fish, Jesus ordered that these be distributed as well. When
everyone had eaten their fill, the leftovers were gathered and they
filled seven baskets. Jesus was first thankful for what little they had;
only then could the crowd be thankful for the feast.

FOCUSING ON WHAT IS PRESENT

Like the disciples, we tend to focus more on what we don't have,
what we can't do and where we fall short. We often define and ap-
praise our faith communities the same way. What is absent can
obscure what is present. This happens when we focus more on
needs than assets. It is also one of the pitfalls of the "visionary
dreamer." There is a devastating passage about visionary dreamers
in Dietrich Bonhoeffer's *Life Together*. The visionary dreamer is
proud and pretentious. He fashions the ideal of community in his
head and then "demands that it be realized by God, by others, and
by himself." Because the visionary dreamer makes the rules, he also
sits as judge over God and men. "He acts as if he is the creator of
the Christian community, as if his dream binds men together."
When things don't go according to plan, he calls the effort a failure.
Gratitude leaves no room for this kind of visionary dreaming, as
Bonhoeffer makes plain:

> Because God has already laid the only foundation of our fel-
> lowship, because God has bound us together in one body with
> other Christians in Jesus Christ, long before we entered into
> common life with them, we enter into that common life not
> as demanders but as thankful recipients. We thank God for
> giving us brethren who live by his call, by his forgiveness, and
> his promise. We do not complain of what God does not give
> us; we rather thank God for what he does give us daily.

And is not what has been given us enough: brothers, who will go on living with us through sin and need under the blessing of his grace? Is the divine gift of Christian fellowship anything less than this, any day, even the most difficult and distressing day?[11]

Rather than emphasizing what's not there, the church should focus on what is. The work of Slow Church is, in part, to help people discern their gifts, provide opportunities for people to publicly praise God for them and support them as they exercise those gifts—regifting them for God's glory.

Asset mapping in congregations. The process of asset mapping is one tool church communities can use to sharpen their focus on available assets, the gifts that God has already provided. In his helpful book *The Power of Asset Mapping: How Your Congregation Can Act on Its Gifts,* Luther Snow names five different types of assets that a congregation should consider:

- *Physical assets:* things that you can touch and see, from land and equipment to natural beauty and the environment

- *Individual assets:* the talents, skills and experiences of individuals

- *Associational assets:* voluntary groups and networks of people (both formal and informal)

- *Institutions:* agencies, corporations and other organizations with budgets and staff (both nonprofit and for profit)

- *Economic assets:* community assets involving money, such as our spending power, our investments and our capacity to produce goods and services for money[12]

The process of asset mapping not only helps us recognize the assets in these categories, it helps us connect the dots to make these assets work together for the flourishing of our neighborhoods. In short, asset mapping is a way to initiate conversations about the gifts and resources we have as church communities and about imagining new ways to organize and catalyze these gifts.

Appreciative inquiry. Another tool for cultivating gratitude in our church communities is appreciative inquiry (AI), a process for organizational change rooted in grateful reflection on the organization's shared history. Mark Lau Branson, in his book *Memories, Hopes and Conversations: Appreciative Inquiry and Congregational Change,* says, "The thesis of Appreciative Inquiry is that an organization, such as a church, can be recreated by its conversations. And if that new creation is to feature the most life-giving forces and forms possible, then the conversations must be shaped by appreciative questions."[13] Drawing upon gratitude for God's past work in the congregation, AI revolves around five processes:

1. Choose the positive as the focus of inquiry

2. Inquire into stories of life-giving forces

3. Locate themes that appear in the stories and select topics for further inquiry

4. Create shared images for a preferred future

5. Find innovative ways to create that future[14]

Branson's book is structured around the story of his own congregation, First Presbyterian Church of Altadena, and how they have been transformed by their engagements with AI. When Branson started working with the church, it was struggling. It had just lost a pastor and faced significant divisions in leadership and theology. The demographics of the neighborhood surrounding the church were changing, which stirred up confusion in the congregation. "Even with a few newcomers," Branson concludes, "there was no shared vision, no common hope of an enlivened future."[15] Over a period of two years, the church immersed itself in appreciative reflection on its history and theology. These conversations dramatically revitalized the life of that church: "Members are [now] more empowered, imaginations are more engaged, and new initiatives are being welcomed. The tone, the mood of the church is one of expectancy, knowing we have hard work to do while also confident that we are in the midst of generative trajectories."[16]

ASSET-BASED COMMUNITY DEVELOPMENT

Congregations like First Presbyterian Church of Altadena that are gratefully engaged with the story of what God is doing in their midst are in the process of learning to cultivate community. In agriculture, cultivation is an act of collaboration between the divine and the human. Ultimately, plants and animals are gifts from God, but through attentive breeding or pollination and care, humans can cultivate advantageous strains of a particular plant or animal. To cultivate a piece of land is to prepare it for sowing, paying special attention to the health and fertility of the soil. Similarly, the cultivation of community, involves organizing the gifts God has provided in our fellow church members and neighbors in ways that promote the flourishing of community in the church and the neighborhood.

In the work of cultivating community, we have found the language and ideas of Asset-Based Community Development (ABCD) to be particularly helpful. ABCD is based on the community organizing and community development work of John McKnight and John Kretzmann, and is introduced most thoroughly in the book these two coauthored, *Building Communities from the Inside Out*. McKnight and Kretzmann contrast asset-based development with needs-based development, which they sometimes call the "deficiency model." Needs-based development is particularly tempting in devastated communities such as struggling rural towns or inner-city neighborhoods, as well as a growing number of older suburban communities where some prominent needs are on bold display. But the deficiency model tends to define neighbors by their needs, and the solutions it offers can leave neighbors increasingly reliant on outside service providers. Not only does this needs-based approach fragment traditional care relationships of neighbors, it ignores the strengths and capacities that are already present. It also tends to be specialist-driven, which means "the relationships that count for most local residents are no longer those inside the community, those neighbor-to-neighbor links of mutual support and problem solving." Focusing on needs often "deepens the cycle of dependence," which can lead to feelings of powerlessness and hopelessness.[17]

Asset-based development, in contrast, seeks to empower neighbors and leverage their skills to the benefit of the whole community. ABCD is defined by three characteristics: (1) It starts with what is present, not what is absent. (2) It is internally focused, emphasizing the "agenda building and problem-solving capacities of local residents, local associations and local institutions" and "the primacy of local definition, investment, creativity, hope and control." (3) It is relationship driven. ABCD leaders must "constantly build and rebuild the relationships between and among local residents, local associations and local institutions."[18]

At Englewood Christian Church, we have been engaged in community development work for almost two decades. This work is driven by an asset-based philosophy, which we have come to see as a concrete practice of gratitude. We start with the assets that are already in place in the neighborhood and leverage those to provide vision and resources for addressing challenging issues. For instance, our neighborhood has a high rate of abandoned properties. This is usually viewed as problematic. For us, however, these properties were assets, which we gratefully acquired for little or no cost and fixed up for members of our congregation or other neighbors. We recently had the opportunity to convert the school building next door to our church into thirty-two units of mixed-income houses. When someone moves into the building, we sit down with him or her and listen to what they are gifted at or passionate about. Even if a person has very visible struggles, we strive to practice gratitude by receiving that person as a gift and working with him or her to connect their skills and gifts with opportunities in the neighborhood where they would be appreciated. We helped an artist get his work displayed in the building's community room. Several residents work part time keeping the building clean. Another resident, working in conjunction with our community development corporation, has started an amazing tamale restaurant on our block. Gratitude is foundational to our life together. We strive to receive one another, our neighbors and our place as gifts of God intended not for our private good as individuals or as a church but for God's work of reconciliation in helping our place to heal and flourish.

GRATITUDE AND COMMUNITY LIFE

Researchers have found that the happiest people also tend to be the most grateful. But while this might seem obvious at first, there's an interesting twist. These folks aren't grateful for being happy; they are happy because they have been intentional about cultivating a life of gratitude. We have a hunch that something very similar might be true of our faith communities: the most joyful churches are probably the ones that have been intentional about making space for gratitude.

What would it look like for us to incorporate gratitude into our life together? The answers to that question are as numerous and diverse as our churches. Perhaps we can be inspired by the story of the ark being brought to Jerusalem and placed in the tent King David had pitched for it. In this "vibrant picture of the various dimensions of the practice of gratitude within worship,"[19] we see that David appointed certain people to invoke, thank and praise the God of Israel, to make burnt offerings according to God's commands, to play music and to sing liturgies of praise.

Years ago someone told me (John) that they could tell how in love I was with my wife because of the way I "spoke well" of her when she wasn't in the room. Think of how important it is, then, for the church—the bride of Christ—to speak well of the Bridegroom to each other, and to share stories about God's marvelous works and faithfulness! One of the most compelling images in all of Scripture is in 2 Chronicles 5. There we see that when the trumpeters and singers made themselves heard in unison, singing praise to God—"For he is good, for his steadfast love endures forever"—the house of the Lord was filled with a cloud, "for the glory of the LORD filled the house of God" (vv. 11-14). This is possible for our churches as well. Our sanctuaries, school gyms or living rooms—wherever we gather to speak well of God—might not be filled with a cloud, but when we remember God's abundant provision, our faith communities will be filled with a joyful overflowing of the Spirit of God.

Cincinnati's Vineyard Central is one church that has long-standing practices of expressing gratitude by blessing and affirming its members. When new members join the church, others in the church bless the new members and commission them to live into the fullness of the congregation's membership covenant. Recently, the church has been inviting their children to offer a blessing, a prayer or another piece of food to each member after they partake of the elements of Communion. "Having the children serve and bless adults in this extended Eucharist feast," says pastor Joshua Stoxen, "has been a joyful and tangible reminder of what it means to humbly receive the Kingdom as little children." This practice is not only a blessing to the adult members of the church, it is a compelling expression of gratitude for the children in the congregation, who are not marginalized but rather encouraged to participate.

Slow churches can incorporate gratitude into many facets of community life, including times of discernment and prayer and in the midst of our community business. Shared meals are infused with a spirit of gratitude. What better time to remember God's provision than when we are surrounded by good food and good friends? Gratitude is also intimately connected to sabbath rest and delight. "Gratitude and wonder are squeezed out when our lives are packed full with busyness and responsibilities," writes Christine Pohl.

"There is simply no room, no time to notice. We experience God's gifts when we pause long enough to notice them."[20]

Pohl also suggests having "rituals of exit" like those we have for beginnings.[21] There are many reasons why people leave a church, and many departures are surrounded by mystery and speculation and gossip. Sometimes a family leaves a church and only the elders know why. There are circumstances where this is warranted. And at other times, the people who are leaving prefer that the reasons not be made public. But wouldn't it better if, whenever possible, we came together to say goodbye, to bless our departing friends on their journey and to say thank you for all the ways they have touched our lives?

Finally, we encourage every faith community to research and tell the history of their church and neighborhood. This history is a record of good times and bad, of birth and death, marriage and divorce, of struggles and tragedies and unexpected blessings, and of the many ways our communities have been touched by the changing tide of events. When we learn, rehearse and recite that story, what will emerge is our own psalm of thanksgiving.

CONVERSATION STARTERS

1. What are some practices of gratitude that you have in your church community? Similarly, what are your practices of celebration? How do you acknowledge and "rejoice with those who rejoice"?

2. Think back over your history in the congregation. Describe a time when you felt most alive and energized. Who was involved, what happened and why was it energizing to you?

3. What is the most life-giving virtue of your congregation? Tell stories from your life together that reflect that virtue.[22]

10

Hospitality

Generously Sharing God's Abundance

*We learn the skills of hospitality in small increments
of daily faithfulness. The moral life is much less about dramatic
gestures than it is about steady work—faithfulness undergirded by
prayer and sustained by grace. The surprise is how often it is
accompanied by mystery, blessing, and joy.*

Christine Pohl, *Sojourners magazine*
(July-August 1999)

❧

The son of the governor general of Canada, Jean Vanier was born into a life of privilege and promise. After a term in the Royal Navy, he attended university and eventually earned a doctorate in moral philosophy from the Institut Catholique in Paris. He went home to Canada intending to begin his career as a professor and scholar. But Vanier's life changed direction when he returned to France in 1963 at the invitation of Father Thomas Philippe, a Dominican priest who had mentored Vanier in college. Father Thomas, who was now serving as a chaplain for about thirty people with disabilities, urged Vanier to do something for people with developmental disabilities.

Vanier was distressed by the living conditions of many disabled people in France. There was one especially disturbing visit to an asylum south of Paris where approximately eighty disabled men lived amid chaos and violence in two concrete dormitories. They had no work. They spent much of their day going around in circles. One man, Dany, spent his life in a cellar and spat at anyone who approached him. Vanier reflected later, "There was something terrifying about it but at the same time something difficult to touch, something profoundly of God. . . . In places of horror there is a kind of presence of God. Peace and chaos—one is frightened yet captivated."[1]

In 1964, Vanier invited two men with disabilities to live with him in a little home in Trosly-Breuil. He called the house L'Arche, after Noah's ark, and he still lives there fifty years later. L'Arche was an alternative to institutions that locked away people with disabilities as something to be ashamed of or as burdens too great to bear. Vanier's vision was for communities of people with and without disabilities living in covenant together, sharing life and recognizing each other as beloved children of God with something uniquely important to contribute. Over the past half-century, Vanier has traveled around the world with this message, and today there are 130 L'Arche communities in thirty countries on six continents.

Jean Vanier has written: "In the midst of all the violence and corruption of the world God invites us today to create new places of belonging, places of sharing, of peace and of kindness, places where no-one needs to defend himself or herself; places where each one is loved and accepted with one's own fragility, abilities and disabilities. This is my vision for our churches: *that they become places of belonging, places of sharing.*"[2]

Vanier's vision of churches as communities defined by belonging and sharing is an inspiration to the slow church economy we have described so far. God provides abundantly for creation, and particularly for the reconciling work that is the mission of God in the world. As we discussed in the previous chapter, we respond to God's abundant generosity with gratitude, and then, as Vanier has noted, we embody our gratitude by following God's example and generously sharing the resources that we have been given.

The superabundance of God's kingdom is not intended for our own indulgence, but rather as a sign of the gospel to be shared freely. As an expression of gratitude for the superabundant provision of God, we share generously to meet the needs that arise among the brothers and sisters of our church community, as well as those in our neighborhoods. Like the church community in Jerusalem in the days after Pentecost, there shouldn't be a needy one among us. In our slowness, we can be attentive to the needs that arise around us, recognizing them sometimes even before they are spoken.

When the topics of generosity and sharing arise in conversation, our minds often jump to giving money. Although giving money is essential to the redemptive work of churches and nonprofits and shouldn't be discouraged, many of our systems of philanthropy promote sharing in a way that keeps the giver well removed from the recipient. For churches, one of the most transformative, and intimate, forms of generosity is hospitality: sharing our homes, our tables and ourselves with others, particularly strangers.

THE OTHERNESS OF GOD'S PEOPLE

Hospitality was foundational to morality in the ancient Near East, in part because it was so necessary for survival. Hardships in the volatile region included war and conquest, vulnerability to robbery and assault, and the deep, mostly uncrossable economic chasm between the peasants and the elite. There was famine, crop failures and drought, including one cycle of famine and drought so severe that it seems to have precipitated a two-hundred-year "dark age" in Egypt. Illness was sometimes attributed to immorality or demon possession, which often segregated the sick from the rest of the community. Widows and orphans could be similarly displaced from vital family and social structures. Hospitality was therefore often carefully bounded and reciprocal. For example, it was customary in many desert cultures to grant anyone who asked three days of hospitality. Water was provided for foot washing. A meal was prepared. You had a roof over your head. Care and security were given to friends, strangers and even enemies, because you might be the one requesting hospitality next time.

Part of what distinguished the hospitality of ancient Israel—and later the hospitality of the first Christians—from that of its neighbors is that it was rooted in the "otherness" of Israel and, ultimately, in the hospitality of God. Abraham presented himself as a stranger to the Hittites (Gen 23:4). Joseph's father and brothers presented themselves to Pharaoh as sojourners escaping famine (Gen 47:4, 9). King David acknowledged the hospitality of God when he announced to an assembly that his son Solomon would be building the temple. David offered burnt offerings and cried out to God, "Blessed are you, O LORD, the God of our ancestor Israel, forever and ever. . . . But who am I, and what is my people, that we should be able to make this freewill offering? For all things come from you, and of your own have we given you. For we are aliens and transients before you, as were all our ancestors" (1 Chron 29:10, 14-15). The hospitality of God is also connected to the Jubilee year, which we discussed earlier: "The land shall not be sold in perpetuity, for the land is mine; with me you are but aliens and tenants. Throughout the land that you hold, you shall provide for the redemption of the land" (Lev 25:23-24).

"The Bible makes the experience of marginality normative for the people of God," Christine Pohl writes in *Making Room*, her essential book on recovering the tradition of Christian hospitality. "For the Israelites and the early Christians, understanding themselves as aliens and sojourners was a reminder of their dependence on God."[3] Pohl describes how Israel's code of hospitality included special mention of resident aliens, making provisions for their welfare and gradually folding them permanently into the life of the people.

Compassion for the resident alien was tied to Israel's past. "You shall not oppress a resident alien; you know the heart of an alien, for you were aliens in the land of Egypt" (Ex 23:9). This exhortation is repeated in Leviticus:

> When an alien resides with you in your land, you shall not oppress the alien. The alien who resides with you shall be to you as the citizen among you; you shall love the alien as yourself, for you were aliens in the land of Egypt: I am the LORD your God. (19:33-34)

Pohl writes that "Israel's experience of vulnerability and dependence was expected to yield a sympathetic and gracious treatment of the vulnerable aliens in its own land."[4] It's worth asking ourselves whether we have the cultural memory to recall times when our families, ancestors, churches and neighborhoods were vulnerable and whether we have the imagination to translate those memories into compassionate care for the vulnerable around us now. Several times throughout this book we've mentioned how transformative it can be to write the story of our church and neighborhoods. I (John) have even seen firsthand what happens when controversial aspects of a church's past are left unexplored or unacknowledged. The church's past remains bathed in soft, hagiographic light; meanwhile, the people who might find safety and belonging from such an honest inquiry remain obscured by the shadows.

"YOU DID IT UNTO ME"

If consideration for the resident alien was what made Israel's hospitality unique, what made the hospitality of the early Christian church distinct in its time was that it went out of its way to include people who couldn't possibly reciprocate. Luke 14 tells of the time Jesus went to the house of a leader of the Pharisees to eat a meal on the sabbath. When Jesus noticed how some of the other guests were jockeying for seats of honor at the table, he told them a couple parables.

First, Jesus told the guests that when they are invited to a wedding banquet they shouldn't choose a place of honor; they should choose the lowest place, so that the host can honor them in front of everyone by saying, "Friend, move up higher." Jesus said, "For all who exalt themselves will be humbled, and those who humble themselves will be exalted." Then Jesus said to the host that when he gives a luncheon or dinner, he shouldn't invite friends, family and rich neighbors—the people who can pay him back. Instead, he should "invite the poor, the crippled, the lame, and the blind. And you be will be blessed, because they cannot repay you, for you will be repaid at the resurrection of the righteous" (Lk 14:10-14).

The second parable Jesus told is about a man who prepared a big feast and sent out invitations to many people. But all the invitees had some excuse for why they couldn't come: they had to check on property or livestock, or they begged off for family reasons. This made the host angry so he opened his house to the poor, crippled, lame and blind. When he saw there was still room at the table, he sent one of his slaves out into the streets to compel perfect strangers to come join the party. "For I tell you," said the host, "none of those who were invited will taste my dinner" (Lk 14:24).

Christians spend too much time "deciding" who *can't* be included at the dinner party. In contrast, we believe it's our responsibility and privilege as followers of Jesus to add chairs to the table, not take them away,[5] almost compelling the Host to make more room as we eagerly spread the good news of God's abundant hospitality among our neighbors. Just as Jesus frequented the meals and parties of his neighbors, we too should make it a priority to eat and relax often with our neighbors.

The teaching that seems to have most inspired the counter-cultural hospitality of the early church is the famous passage about the sheep and the goats. At the very end of his last discourse in the book of Matthew, Jesus said:

Then the king will say to those at his right hand, "Come, you that are blessed by my Father, inherit the kingdom prepared for you from the foundation of the world; for I was hungry and you gave me food, I was thirsty and you gave me something to drink, I was a stranger and you welcomed me, I was naked and you gave me clothing, I was sick and you took care of me, I was in prison and you visited me." Then the righteous will answer him, "Lord, when was it that we saw you hungry and gave you food, or thirsty and gave you something to drink? And when was it that we saw you a stranger and welcomed you, or naked and gave you clothing? And when was it that we saw you sick or in prison and visited you?" And the king will answer them, "Truly I tell you, just as you did it to one of the least of these who are members of my family, you did it to me." (25:34-40)

"You did it unto me" is a stunning picture of the upside-down kingdom. The world is God's and everything in it. We live by divine hospitality. And yet we are given the opportunity—even the command—to offer hospitality to God by caring for the people who are the most vulnerable.

Mother Teresa said, "I see Jesus in every human being. I say to myself, this is hungry Jesus, I must feed him. This is sick Jesus. This one has leprosy or gangrene; I must wash him and tend to him. I serve because I love Jesus."

Mother Teresa took "you did it unto me" at face value, as did many in the early church. Clement of Alexandria (ca. 150–ca. 215) applied the standards of Christian hospitality to the relationships of slaves and masters. An anonymous writer urged Christians to offer hospitality to the image of God (the hungry, naked, thirsty, stranger and prisoner) as an extension of worship. Lactantius (ca. 240–320) said that proper hospitality to the poor and stranger extended even to the grave by offering them a proper burial. St.

Gregory of Nyssa (330–395) said, "The stranger, those who are naked, without food, infirm and imprisoned are the ones the Gospel intends for you." St. Benedict (480–550) said in his *Rule* for monks that all guests to the monastery must be received like Christ. The biographer of St. John the Almsgiver (ca. 550–616) said that the Patriarch of Alexandria upended traditional notions of power by calling the "poor and beggars" his "masters and helpers." He even gave a double portion of alms to a man whom he knew to be a false beggar, saying, "perchance it is my Christ and He is making trial of me."[6]

Hospitality was so important to the early church that it was a test of character (1 Tim 5:10) and a requirement for leadership (1 Tim 3:2; Tit 1:8). In fact, the hospitality of Christians was well known enough that in the year 362 the Emperor Julian, who wanted to revive Roman values and Hellenic faith, told his high priest (referring to Christians as "atheists"): "Why do we not observe that it is their benevolence to strangers, their care for the graves of the dead and the pretended holiness of their lives that have done most to increase atheism?" He went on, "For it is disgraceful that, when no Jew ever has to beg, and the impious Galilaeans [Christians] support not only their own poor but ours as well, all men see that our people lack aid from us."[7]

LOVE OF THE STRANGER

The words translated as "hospitality" or "hospitable" in the New Testament are often variations on the Greek *philoxenia,* which literally means "love of the stranger." Today, when we hear the word "hospitality" we're less likely to think of hospitality as love shown toward the stranger and more likely to think of it as an industry. In fact, the hospitality industry—which includes hotels, lodging and accommodations, restaurants and food service—is the world's fastest growing industry, earning 3.4 trillion dollars annually. It's also the largest private employer in the United States. Interestingly, the federal government lumps the hospitality industry in with "leisure" (Bureau of Labor Statistics) and "travel and tourism" (Department of Commerce), both of which imply freedom from normal obligations and a profit motive, and which indicates how far we have drifted from the idea of the subversive, often invisible *dailyness* of early Christian hospitality.

So much modern hospitality has become privatized. It has also become specialized. The acts of mercy often associated with hospitality have now been outsourced to charitable organizations, for-profits, ministries and the government. Sick people go to the hospital. The pilgrim goes to a hostel. The homeless go to a shelter. The hungry go to a soup kitchen or food bank. The poor receive financial assistance from the government in the form of welfare checks and food stamps. These are all vital institutions that deserve to be supported and even strengthened. But they can't take the place of person-to-person hospitality. Specialized care runs the risk of becoming too targeted, so focused on *doing something* about one particular problem that it can miss out on the holistic (and mutual) benefits of *being with* the person in need.

Which brings us to a third point about modern hospitality: it can keep the guest and host at arm's length from one another. In the Christian tradition of hospitality, even as the host is blessing the guest, the guest is blessing the host. The relationship is paramount. Hospitality isn't a transaction or impersonal charity; it is seeing in the other the image of God, connecting to that uniquely precious person, and giving them the space and security they need to reveal their authentic self. The hosts also leave themselves vulnerable enough to reveal their own authentic selves.

We live in a culture that is often characterized by disingenuousness, competition and ulterior motives. But in a space where true belonging is possible, even an enemy can become a friend. Here we see most clearly that all our attempts at hospitality are rooted in the greatest act of hospitality, the death and resurrection of Jesus, which brought us into the family of God. According to Romans 5:10, "while we were enemies, we were reconciled to God by the death of the Son." First Peter 2:10 says, "Once you were not a people, but now you are God's people; once you had not received mercy, but now you have received mercy." And Jesus told his disciples:

> This is my commandment, that you love one another as I have loved you. No one has greater love than this, to lay down one's life for one's friends. You are my friends if you do what I command you. I do not call you servants any longer, because the servant does not know what the master is doing; but I have called you friends, because I have made known to you everything that I have heard from my Father. You did not choose me but I chose you. . . . I am giving you these commands so that you may love one another. (Jn 15:12-17)

Christine Pohl writes in *Making Room* that Jesus connected hospitality, grace and sacrifice. "He is himself both host and meal—the very source of life." Referring to the Eucharist, she says, "As we remember the cost of our welcome, Christ's body and shed blood, we also celebrate the reconciliation and relationship available to us because of his blood and sacrifice and through his hospitality." A shared meal is thus "the activity most closely tied to the reality of God's Kingdom" as well as the "most basic expression of hospitality."[8]

And it's true: sharing a meal with someone is one of the most intimate things we can do. We open our home, prepare and serve our food, and settle in around a table together to pray, eat, laugh, cry, reconcile, catch up or introduce ourselves, and hear each other's stories. A shared meal is characterized by vulnerability, social recognition, proximity and revelation. So tied is the breaking of bread to the recognition of Jesus in our midst that it was only in the context of a meal that the two disciples realized the stranger they had been traveling with on the road to Emmaus was the resurrected Christ (Lk 24:13-32).

Finding ways to eat together is vitally important for faith communities. Englewood Christian Church has been hosting weekly Wednesday night hospitality dinners for almost a decade. It creates a space for them to receive others—fellow church members, families who are part of the daycare and other neighbors—as gifts from God and to share food. Silverton Friends holds a potluck before every business meeting, which has the added effect of strengthening the bonds of community before making hard decisions (always on a consensus basis) or discussing contentious issues.

In addition, multiple churches in Silverton are involved in providing twice-weekly community meals. On Monday evening, Oak Street Church hosts a meal that serves over a hundred people from all walks of life. On Wednesday, several churches—including Silverton Friends—collaborate to put on Community Dinner at First Christian Church. Wednesday Community Dinner started in 2008 as a way of providing a free weekly meal during tough economic times. The goal was to serve a spaghetti dinner to maybe twenty-five people. Five years later, over four hundred people are served each week (in a town of ten thousand), including rich and poor, employed and unemployed, the homeless, local politicians, religious and not, families, the very young and the very old—all sitting together at small tables. The pastor of First Christian Church told one of the local papers in 2012, "We want our actions to speak louder than our words. We want God's love to radiate and we want to be a place open to all and where all feel comfortable coming."[9] Some nights a local teenager plays classical music on an upright piano, other nights an older man walks around serenading strangers on his accordion. Smiling faces say hello and help serve. Often, little kids jump in to help wipe down tables. And the bread is always homemade. Over seventy-five thousand meals have been served at First Christian Church since 2008, and, miraculously, they have never run out of food. It really is extraordinary.

HOSPITALITY AND McDONALDIZATION

Hopefully it is obvious by now that Christian hospitality is a direct challenge to the most dehumanizing aspects of McDonaldization. The ethics of the assembly line turns people into robots, requiring them to lay down their skills, talents and creativity and instead repeatedly perform a few simplified tasks. In contrast, as we've seen, the best hospitality provides safe space for the guest and host to "reveal their most precious gifts and bring new life to each other."[10]

Elizabeth Newman has written that Christian hospitality compels us to give up *predictability* and *control* (both hallmarks of McDonaldization) "because it acknowledges that God comes among us in surprising and strange ways that we can never fully predict or domesticate."[11] Indeed, as another scholar has noted, the three most significant events in Christian history were all accompanied by the arrival of a mysterious stranger: Christmas (the infant born in a barn), Easter (the man on the road to Emmaus) and Pentecost (the rushing wind of the Holy Spirit).[12] Jesus himself seems to have been homeless for most of his ministry years (Lk 9:58), choosing to rely on the hospitality of others.

Hospitality also challenges the cult of speed. Newman says that Christian hospitality

> allows time to be patient and vulnerable with others. Such hospitality does not fit with the instantaneous demands of the market. . . . Whereas the global market aims for efficiency and speed, Christian hospitality is content to wait, to take time, to apparently do nothing if need be, since the aim is to be in God's abundant time of giving and receiving rather than in efficient, productive time.[13]

Because the market evaluates people in terms of their production and consumption, a society that nearly deifies the market's "invisible hand" can start to value people based on the same criteria.

Christian hospitality, in contrast, accepts people wholly as they are, with no advantage seeking or expectation of reciprocity, no litmus test of economic worth or usefulness. A person's worth is derived permanently and unequivocally from their status as the precious handiwork of God. Thus, our hospitality should emerge as we seek to follow the Bible's ordinary yet deeply radical call to embrace the other.

Who is the "other" in our culture? Who are the traditionally overlooked people we will encounter today when we slow down long enough to see people as Jesus saw them? The poor—the very poor, the barely getting by, the people who can't keep their heads above water very much longer. The unemployed and the under-employed. The hungry or food insecure. Single parents doing heroic work but who could use a helping hand. Orphans and foster children, widows and widowers. Immigrants (undocumented or otherwise), the homeless and the refugees. An enemy. The imprisoned, paroled and the convicted sex offender. The racial and ethnic "other." Social minorities. The very young and the very old. College students far from home. Patients. The disabled. The mentally ill. The sick and the dying and the dead. Our hospitality should extend beyond those who are like us and beyond those who can reciprocate, to the people God brings our way—folks who are beloved children of God, just like us.

Hospitality also challenges the placelessness that is so endemic in modern society. This placelessness takes many forms, including the transience and hypermobility we talked about earlier, homelessness, immigration and displacement. Many experts believe the number of refugees will skyrocket over the next several decades as "environmental migrants" move to escape the worst effects of climate change, water shortages and other natural crises.

We see placelessness in the desecrated places—the strip-mined mountains, industrial wastelands and remnants of city blocks that were abused during their lifetime and abandoned once they ceased to be useful or desirable.

Placelessness can also come in the form of "nonplaces." In the late 1970s, a Canadian geographer named Edward Relph wrote an influential book that described placelessness as "the casual eradication of distinctive places and the making of standardized landscapes."[14] Relph describes two main sources of placelessness: *kitsch*, or the uncritical acceptance of mass values, and *technique*, which evaluates everything by the overriding concerns of efficiency and objectivity. This results in the "undermining of place for both individuals and cultures and the casual replacement of the diverse and significant places of the world with anonymous spaces and exchangeable environments."[15] Malls, chain stores and even subdivisions all look the same from one town and city to the next. They are so familiar, and so pervasive, that the effect can be (perhaps even *should* be) dizzying.

Hospitality connects us to a place, because while hospitality can happen pretty much anywhere, it has to happen *somewhere*. Hospitality requires proximity, and by definition, proximity implies nearness in space, time or relationship—all of which assume certain limits. Accepting this boundedness, we begin the work of turning *space* into a *place* of belonging.

We should be generous with our use of the facilities God has given our faith communities. The homes we own, as individuals or as the church, are not just our private residences but are God-given resources to be shared. Englewood Christian Church has a hospitality house next door to the church building where individuals, families and groups are welcomed when it is available. This house provides a space in which guests can stay for days or weeks, and in which the church can get to know them. Families in the church have opened their homes to short- or long-term guests, and even occasionally to homeless neighbors. Englewood and Silverton Friends invite and encourage community groups of all sorts to meet in their buildings, often allowing use of the space at no cost. Silverton Friends hosts a MOPs (Mothers of Preschoolers) group, financial wellness courses, and an *intercambio* language and culture exchange for young native English and Spanish speakers. There is also a K-8 Christian school on campus. Over the last decade, a number of small nonprofits have had their offices in the building of Englewood Christian Church, in addition to the daycare and all the businesses of its community development corporation. Hardly a night or weekend goes by when there is not at least one group meeting in our buildings.

That being said, for many people, sanctuaries—which used to be literal places of refuge, beyond the reach of unjust secular laws—may never be places of belonging. Churches can carry baggage of abuse, neglect, hypocrisy, judgmentalism, misogyny, homophobia, offensive politics or a general distrust of institutions. "They need to get over it," we've heard some Christians say in response—but this is inconsistent with Christian hospitality, which compels us to meet people as they are and offer them safety and security and support. For this reason, becoming a more hospitable people will probably mean looking beyond our church walls. We'll have to get comfortable with a more porous dividing line between the public and private. And we'll probably need to experiment with ways to connect the church to our homes. As many scholars, missiologists, pastors and church planters have noted, the home was "the essential sphere for hospitality" and the primary, practical medium through which the early church spread (Acts 20:20).[16]

Just as Christ drew close to humanity in the incarnation, generously sharing our spaces as churches and individuals is a way in which we are drawn closer together. In the final chapter, we will explore one important form of hospitality—eating together—with a special focus on the transformative dynamics of dinner table conversation.

CONVERSATION STARTERS

1. What are your practices of hospitality as a congregation? How do you make people feel welcome and help them feel like they belong to your church community—particularly people who are outside the typical demographics of your congregation?

2. In what ways does your church extend hospitality to neighbors who might never attend a church service or activity? Have members invited neighbors over for meals and conversation? Does the church allow neighborhood groups to use its facilities? Share stories of extending hospitality to neighbors, and discuss what you have learned from these experiences.

3. In what ways are resources—homes, cars, skills, tools and so on—shared among members of your congregation? How can you encourage and facilitate more sharing of resources?

11

Dinner Table Conversation as a Way of Being Church

*The Kingdom of God is not in the
wisdom of the world, nor in eloquence,
but in the faith of the cross and in
the virtue of dialogue.*

St. Cyprian

The vision of life we tried to describe over the course of this book is one that is both holistic in its scope and slow and attentive in its praxis. There is a temptation to emphasize one of these facets of Slow Church over the other. For example, we can get so consumed by the broadness of God's mission of reconciliation that we become frantic in our efforts to join in. We can also get so comfortable with the pleasures of our slow life together that we lose sight of God's reconciling work beyond our own community. Eugene Peterson describes this same tension in his examination of the church as a political community. On one end of the spectrum, we lose sight of our identity in Christ and are seduced by the coercive political means of the world. "Instead of riding that silly donkey, [we are tempted to believe that] Jesus should have charged up to Jerusalem on a stallion and let a few heads roll." The other extreme, he says, "is to give up the political and have a nice little fellowship—cultivate a faith that more or less abandons the world of government, economics, culture, and society."[1]

How do we abide in the tension between these two poles? One way is to develop patterns of meeting and being together that immerse us in the fullness of our calling to the Way. This creates space for facing the complexities of life together and conversationally discerning what the next steps of faithfulness should be. Specifically, we challenge you to imagine what our common life would look like if it were centered around (a) eating together at the table and (b) the slow, eucharistic conversation that convivial feasting encourages.

Though we're focusing here on two specific aspects of the common meal—eating together and conversation—we aren't proposing a technique that produces sure and automatic results. We're offering an image to spark our imaginations. In fact, in some communities, such as those with small children, mealtime might not allow for much conversation. Jonathan Wilson-Hartgrove has said that his Rutba House community often welcomes visitors who come with romanticized ideas of the common meal but leave disappointed because mealtime was so loud and chaotic that it made sustained conversation difficult. Eating together and conversing together are both vital practices of a slow church community, and it seems natural for them to be interwoven. But in practice this might not always be possible. Some communities might have to develop them separately.

THE CULTURE OF THE TABLE

For centuries, sharing meals as families, extended families or social groups has been a cornerstone of culture. It is arguably humankind's most formative social practice. The richness of this practice, however, has been vastly diluted in an age in which television, smartphones and fast food reign supreme. The average family in the United States eats together less often than they did a quarter century ago. Even when we do eat together, the average length of the meal is growing shorter (as little as twenty minutes, by some accounts), and meals are often in front of the TV or in the car.

It's striking that this sharp decrease in sharing meals coincides with an increasingly fractured political culture where people of different perspectives refuse even to talk to one another. Remember the partisan struggles in Congress to raise the debt ceiling in 2011 and 2013? Lawmakers of both major parties seemed to go out of their way to avoid working together for the common good of the country. Many astute observers attributed this breakdown in civility to a lack of eating and socializing together. Citing both Democrats and Republicans, Dan Merica wrote for CNN, "It is a common refrain on the Hill—the idea that if Congress were more social, more buddy-buddy outside the Capitol complex, that it would be more functional in doing the people's work."[2] So if the problem is widely recognized, why don't we see any change in Washington? "What is the incentive for them [the president and Republicans] to foster these relations?" political commentator Nathan Gonzalez has asked. "Their time is valuable, just to be friends for the sake of being friends, I don't know that they have the time."[3]

This is a portrait of a deeply dysfunctional workplace. If we don't have time to share meals and nurture friendships, even with our coworkers, we have ceded too much ground to the cult of speed. Like any false god, the cult of speed requires sacrifices—in this case, human connection and common flourishing. Its bitter fruits are isolation, alienation and the death of conversation. In chapter five, we mentioned sociologist Bill Bishop and his important book, *The Big Sort,* which describes how Americans have been clustering into increasingly homogeneous communities. Bishop's research confirms that we are becoming less capable of civil dialogue with people who are different from us.

We can't help but wonder if there is a correlation between the decline of the family meal and our diminished public discourse. In one of his last books, Fred Rogers, a Presbyterian minister otherwise known as PBS's Mister Rogers, made the poignant observation that "at the dinner table children learn the art of making conversation—how to take turns listening and talking and how to put their ideas into words. Even the vocabulary increases as they learn new words and new ideas from others in the family."[4] Similarly, Michael Pollan has said, "The shared meal is no small thing. It is a foundation of family life, the place where our children learn the art of conversation and acquire the habits of civilization: sharing, listening, taking turns, navigating differences, arguing without offending."[5]

The dinner table is a school for conversation. If Mister Rogers is right (and he usually is) that we learn to think and speak the language of our family at the dinner table, then could a parallel idea be true about our church communities? As we converse as God's family, rooted in particular places, we learn to think and speak theologically in a distinctive vernacular that fits who and where we are. Maybe by recovering the ancient formative practice of the common meal, our churches can bear witness to the possibilities of diverse and peaceable conversation in a deeply fragmented culture.

EATING CHRIST TOGETHER

Consider the Eucharist. Whether we call it Mass, Eucharist, Communion, the Lord's Supper or some other name, the remembrance of Christ's last meal with his disciples gives shape to many of our church gatherings. But the way it is generally practiced can be oversimplified and highly abstracted.

It wasn't always that way. Jesus said, "Do this in remembrance of me" (Lk 22:19). John Howard Yoder asks a simple but pointed question: what does Jesus mean by "this"?

It could refer to the Passover, since that was the feast Jesus and his disciples were celebrating that night. But the Passover was an

annual feast, and the practices of the first Christ-followers demonstrate that the Eucharist was understood to be more than just a
once-per-year remembrance. Similarly, other sources—including
Paul's correction of the Corinthian church (1 Cor 11:17-21)—
indicate that this practice was more than the sacrament of the bread
and the cup as we know them. Yoder thus concludes that the early
church understood that the "meal Jesus blessed that evening and
claimed as his memorial was their *ordinary* partaking together of
food for the body."[6]

Many churches begin sharing meals for social reasons. Meals
are a great time for us to get to know one another on a deeper level
than is possible by just sharing a pew. Delta Community Christian
Church in Lansing, Michigan, began eating together about ten
years ago as a social component of their weekly gathering. But as
they continued the practice and reflected on the prominence of
the table in Scripture, they realized they were entering into a
Christian practice of rich historic significance. Over time, Delta
adopted the practice of bookending its meal with the traditional
eucharistic bread and cup. It is a reminder that the whole meal is
an expression of the sacrificial remembering Jesus instructed his
disciples to practice.

Gathering around the table to share an ordinary meal is literally
a down-to-earth way for us to celebrate together God's provision
and to extend God's care to one another and to our neighbors.
Though the forces of McDonaldization obscure this truth, the food
we share is ultimately a gift of God from the land. We remember in
our meal together the sacrifice of Christ's life, but we are also partaking in the sacrifices of Christ's creation—the death of plants and
animals, as well as the sweat of those who labored to grow, process
and prepare the food. As was the Israelite custom, Jesus gave thanks
to God before offering the bread and wine to his disciples. In all
likelihood, he intoned the familiar Jewish mealtime blessing:
"Blessed art Thou, God, King of the Universe, by whose goodness

we have this bread to share."[7] As we partake in humble gratitude for the sacrifices made on our behalf, we are called to follow after Jesus in offering ourselves as a sacrifice for our brothers and sisters, our neighbors and even our enemies. This is the eucharistic economy Norman Wirzba describes this way: "Eating Jesus and being eaten by him effects the transformation in us so that we can become the food that nurtures and celebrates the world."[8] In sharing an ordinary meal together, these sacrifices move out of the abstract realm of pure symbol and become tangible in the food (and the people) set before us.

The mere logistics of sharing meals as a eucharistic expression plunge us into a sea of practical economic questions related to our shared Christian discipleship. What are we going to eat? Where will it come from, and at what cost to laborers and the environment? How do we treat members who abstain from certain types of food and drink for reasons of allergies or moral convictions? Who is going to do the work needed to prepare, serve and clean up after the meal? Many of the themes described over the course of this book re-emerge in the questions we ask before eating faithfully together.

Food is central to our identity. We are what we eat. Not only does our food sustain and build up our bodies, much of our identity is tied up in the received cultural wisdom about which foods are good and which ones are forbidden. This gives us insight into just how transformative the gospel was when, in Acts 10, God told Peter to share a meal with the Gentile Cornelius. Rachel Marie Stone, in her superb book *Eat with Joy: Redeeming God's Gift of Food*, observes, "Peter was giving up his lifelong foodways—tantamount to his very identity—for the sake of Christ, unifying himself with those he'd always regarded as 'unclean.'"[9]

Our stories of eating together in our church communities might not be as dramatic as this one, but the reality is the same. In the practice of the common table, we submit ourselves to the transformation of Christ, which shapes us into a new culture with a common identity. We need to be attentive to power dynamics too. The apostle Paul dealt with this concern in his letter to the Corinthian church when he addressed the controversial topic of whether that church's members should eat meat that had been sacrificed to idols (1 Cor 8). Paul encourages the Corinthians to be conscientious of each member's diet and the convictions that shape their food practices. Similarly, as we develop habits of eating together we will have to patiently work through our diverse beliefs about what kinds of food are good and healthy. The common meal, however often we celebrate it, forces us to pull our convictions down from the clouds of abstraction and work them out together in our very specific context.

We hasten to add that while we certainly need spaces for eating together as a congregation, shared meals should also be—to a borrow a term from David Fitch—a practice on the move, that is, one that we sometimes engage in as a church community and sometimes in intentional ways with our neighbors. We need both. Eating together as a church community conforms us more closely into the shape of Jesus; eating with our neighbors draws us into God's work of reconciliation. "[We] are to enter the households, work beside people, and sit at tables where we can listen to their stories and enter their dialogue," says missiologist Alan Roxburgh, "and, perhaps catch the wind of the Spirit as he breathes new forms of witness and life in a time grown tired of church conversations."[10]

THE PRACTICE OF CONVERSATION

A church community formed around an ethic that values the quality of faithfulness, an ecology that is attentive to God's reconciliation of all creation, and an economy rooted in a deep trust in God's abundant provision is a far cry from the status quo. That's why Slow Church requires the imagination to go beyond business as usual, new eyes to see what God is already doing in our neighborhoods and the courage to join God there.

Around the table we live into our common identity as brothers and sisters in Christ. Over time and in proximity, our personal imaginations that have been so profoundly shaped under the influence of individualism, materialism and speed will be woven together into a shared imagination that reflects the reconciled diversity of our community.

As we've seen, none of this can be disconnected from our neighbors, the land, the creaturely community, the built environment or any of the particularities of place. When we joyfully and sacrificially submit to one another, the kingdom of love can break through anywhere and everywhere. One practice by which we submit ourselves to one another—transforming our imaginations in the process—is conversation. And it's through conversation that we make decisions together about how best to faithfully embody Christ in our local neighborhood.

Through conversation, we explore the specific questions of how we enter the ethics, ecology and economy of God. We all know that decisions can be made with little or no conversation, and certainly not all top-down decisions are bad. But authoritarian decisions are often made out of concern for efficiency and control. In contrast, a slow church is a conversational church, one that values the gifts and wisdom that God has provided in all its members. Plus, if our goal is to move from being passive consumers of church to active participants in the mission of God in the world, important decisions made without fruitful conversation are unlikely to be sustainable or truly formational.

Sharing meals creates a space where the conversational life of the church community can flourish. If our meals are intended to be expressions of the Eucharist, our dinner table conversations take on new dimensions of meaning. John Nugent, theologian and member of Delta Community Christian Church, reminded Chris recently that any time a community makes decisions together, questions about power are raised, and in questions of power we are re-minded of the self-emptying nature of God's kingdom. Thus, if we are eating and conversing eucharistically, we imitate Christ in de-nying ourselves and our own personal agendas. Heeding the radical call of Jesus to take up our crosses and follow him must be not only *what* we talk about but *how* we talk about it. To the extent that we can't or don't do this, our conversations will likely get off track and serve ends not wholly of the kingdom of God.

Conversation should be an important part of our church's decision-making process. Not every decision requires a long conversation with the full community, but they all require trust, and that is built up in conversation over time. We trust each other into speech, and we listen each other into trust. We let the Holy Spirit knit our lives together into a more mature body—and as with physical bodies, maturity makes some tasks flow more smoothly and effortlessly.

POTLUCK WORSHIP

In eating and conversing together, we enact our identity as the enfleshed Christ. Just as our physical bodies can't move without the ceaseless "conversation" of the parts carried on through the nerves, so the church can't act in coordination without our own habitual conversations.

Not long after Paul used the metaphor of the body to illustrate the church's unity in Christ (1 Cor 12), he implored the Corin-thians to structure their gathering as a sort of conversation. Each member was to come prepared to share "a hymn, a lesson, a reve-lation, a tongue, or an interpretation" (1 Cor 14:26). Tom Stave, the presiding clerk of the Northwest Yearly Meeting of Friends (Quakers)—John's denomination—has given a modern manifes-tation of this the nickname "potluck worship." As the apostle Paul describes it, these offerings were to be shared in a fashion both orderly and interactive. (John Howard Yoder notes that this practice of meeting was the same sort of conversational gathering that was practiced among the community of believers in Jerusalem in Acts 15.) The passage from 1 Corinthians is worth our reflection as we explore what it might mean to be a community centered around eucharistic dinner table conversation.

First, Paul expects members to come prepared to participate. This leaves little room for passive consumption of religious goods and services.

Second, there is a huge variety in the kinds of offerings brought. This reflects Paul's emphasis earlier in the letter that members of the body have diverse gifts. We're often tempted to read 1 Corinthians and think of gifts in a limited way—for example, Sally is a preacher and her gift to the body is her preaching. But this is reductionist. We should instead say that Sally herself, in all her fullness—all her skills, experiences, and even her inadequacies and brokenness—is a gift of God to the church community. God gathers in a place people who together have the gifts and resources needed to embody Christ in the way that place needs to see Christ embodied. To be a slow church is thus to be a local manifestation of Christ, alert both to the diversity of gifts it has been given in its members and to the particularities of the place in which it is located.

DECISION MAKING BY CONSENSUS

Decision making by consensus is one church practice that fits well with Slow Church and particularly with a community life centered around dinner table conversation. The Christian tradition of consensus decision making goes back to the earliest years of the church ("It has seemed good to the Holy Spirit and to us," Acts 15:28), but it has been most commonly associated in recent centuries with Quaker/Friends communities. It was by consensus that the Quakers in the early years of the United States became the first religious community to reject the practice of slavery. I (John) have seen the consensus process up close, as my church has made decisions related to finances, buildings, ministry and the calling of a new pastor. What I most love about consensus is that my church makes sure that every voice is heard—including the young, the old and the disabled—and that all hearts are clear.

Richard Foster says this about Quaker consensus in his classic work *Celebration of Discipline:*

> Facts are only one aspect of the decision-making process and in themselves are not conclusive. The Spirit can lead contrary to the available facts or in accord with them. He will implant a spirit of unity when the right path has been chosen and trouble us with restlessness when we have not heard Him correctly. Unity rather than majority rule is the principle of corporate guidance.[11]

Despite its aims of unity and respect, consensus, like any decision-making process, can be fraught with conflict. But we must disentangle ourselves from competitiveness and even learn to welcome conflict. Observes Parker Palmer, a noted Quaker educator, "In consensus, everyone can win through conflict, as the clash of apparent opposites gives rise to fresh, fuller truth."[12]

Delta Community Christian Church is another church that has been experimenting with consensus decision making. One member describes it as the "most formative practice in their life together." They have adopted consensus as an expression of the eucharistic (self-denying) life they share and as a witness to their unity in Christ. They are intentional about making sure every voice is heard. They regularly do "pulse checks," during which every member is invited to speak his or her heart on the issue at hand. At appropriate pauses in their conversation—whether they are discussing a passage of Scripture or church finances—the conversation will stop and, member by member, each person is given the opportunity to ask clarifying questions or to state their opinion. Some decline to weigh in, but anyone can have their say. As you may imagine, this practice of pulse checking can be time consuming and messy. The initial conversation might get set aside in favor of other important issues that arise through the pulse check. The benefit of this practice, however, is that everyone can contribute, and there is a clear, shared sense of why a decision is made or what issues need to be resolved before moving forward. Although this practice was painstaking at first, they have found that as they mature together in Christ, decisions no longer require the level of effort they once did.

LEARNING TO BE A CONVERSATIONAL CHURCH

At Englewood Christian Church where I (Chris) am a member, the kinds of eucharistic conversation we've described here have been our most formative practice over the last fifteen years. Every Sunday night, we circle up the chairs in a multipurpose room and have an ongoing conversation about who we are in Christ and how we should share life together in our little corner of urban Indianapolis. We don't literally share a meal together at this meeting (although we do at other times throughout the week), and we don't make decisions by consensus, but this meeting has become the heartbeat of our life together.

I came into this conversation about halfway through its life to date, but I'm told that the earliest years were extremely tense and volatile. We didn't know how to talk to each other. We had an array of theological opinions on core issues like Scripture (what it is, what it's for and how we read it) and the role of the church. Fifteen years of conversation have not made us of one mind on all things, but we would agree that we are growing in that direction and slowly learning to trust and respect each other better even when we don't agree.

The Sunday night conversation has been a means of grace to me. It has taught me to slow down. I'm learning to be more attentive to the people around me, and to the specific opportunities and challenges posed by our neighborhood. When I came to Englewood, I was an activist at heart. I wanted to speed through conversations, make decisions and get things done now, regardless of the collateral damage. I've seen enough over the years to know that God is at work in our midst and that things do get done, though maybe not on my timetable. I am learning to be content with slow progress.

SCRIPTURE AND THE DINNER TABLE CONVERSATION

Very little has been said so far about the role of Scripture in eucharistic conversation. Scripture, for the slow church, is like water for a fish. It is our life and our place and our story. The focus of the eucharistic conversation should be on maturing in our faithfulness to the scriptural narrative. We are a hermeneutic community; we interpret Scripture together in our particular time and place. It's important that we see the broadness of our role. Scripture is about the creation, fall and reconciliation of all things, and we are called to bear witness to the fullness of God's work. While our conversation will be rooted in our identity in Christ, it will not (and should not) always be "religious." It may turn to topics such as how we use the land we own, how children should be educated, how best to care for the marginalized among us and so forth. Scripture shouldn't be a sword we use to jab at each other or smite our neighbors. It is instead an improvisational aid, which as we begin to engage as a congregation helps us understand the meaning of our life together.

In the book *Free for All: Rediscovering the Bible in Community*, Tim Conder and Daniel Rhodes describe their Emmaus Way church community in Durham, North Carolina, and the various ways in which they gather to interpret Scripture together. Understanding themselves primarily as an "interpreting community," Conder and Rhodes note how their practices of interpretation have changed their church:

> [We] have developed a passion for the intersection of word
> and community as well as our distinct willingness to hear
> each other's voices. This is not an innate skill. It's a learned

practice that we've worked hard to cultivate. The community expects to be asked to interpret text. They would now be profoundly disappointed if this responsibility were taken away. Though most have admired the Bible . . . and some have expertise in the tools of exegesis, the community passionately believes in the challenge and the privilege to interpret. . . . We believe that many of the strengths of our community are due to this commitment to a community hermeneutic.[13]

Sharing meals, developing common postures and practices, and forging common convictions build trust and intimacy that we believe will ripple outward from the table and find their way into every aspect of our lives. This was the same dynamic at work in the post-Pentecost church at Jerusalem:

Only because [the breaking of bread] was at the center of their life together could it extend into the formation of economic community: "no one claimed for his own use anything that he had" [Acts 4:32]. The "common purse" of the Jerusalem church was not a purse: It was a common table. It arose not as the fruit of speculation about ideal economic relations. . . . The sharing was rather the normal organic extension from table fellowship.[14]

God longs for the transformation and redemption of all creation, which begins in the people God has called. As we slow down our lives and mingle together around the eucharistic table, and as we deny ourselves and become increasingly attentive to the super-abundant gifts of God in our community and place, we will taste the delectable fruits of God's kingdom. We will come to know the abundant life of *shalom* for which we were created!

CONVERSATION STARTERS

1. What practices of eating together does your church have? How is the food provided for those meals? Who prepares the meal?

Who cleans up after the meal? How can you draw more people into the practice of eating together, and especially into the work that those meals require?

2. What spaces does your congregation have for open conversation? How do you gently invite more people into those spaces, especially those who might be wary of conversation? If you have multiple spaces for conversation, to what extent are they in harmony? And if they do not fit together harmoniously, what can you do to make them more so?

3. What practices does your church have of sharing meals with neighbors? Share stories of your experiences eating with neighbors. How could your congregation encourage this practice more broadly?

Conclusion

The extraordinary thing about Slow Church is how ordinary it is. Slow Church is just church—or it should be. We aren't asking people to be Super Christians, to move to a developing nation or to the inner city, or to give away all their money. What we're advocating is that we live more deeply into the ordinary patterns of our lives, considering and talking with others in our church about *how* and *why* we do the things we do.

Slow Church reflects our own longing to experience the subversive, transforming power of God within the day-to-day life of our churches and neighborhoods. The adjectives *subversive* and *transforming* are intentional here, because we are withdrawing our allegiance to a McDonaldized religion that wants to keep the life of faith segmented to Sunday morning services. In a world where God is at work reconciling all creation, everything matters: work, family, friends, place, rest, food, money and, above all, the body of Christ, because the church is the interpretive community through which we make sense of all other facets of life.

One of our favorite poems is by the agrarian writer Liberty Hyde Bailey. It depicts an encounter between a novice poet and a seasoned one. The novice asks the master where he lives, imagining that it must be some amazing place to inspire the "wondrous scenes" portrayed in the master's poetry. But the novice is in for a surprise. In his own words:

He took me by the hand
And led me to my own hearthstone
We paused upon the wonted floor
And silent stood alone—
Till all the space was over-pent
With a magic wonderment;
And I found the Poet's store
On the threshold of my door.[1]

Like the novice poet, the authors of this book stand in magic wonderment. Because right on the threshold of our own doors—in our churches, neighborhoods and homes—God is already at work. Slowing down, we see it, and we hope you can too. Our response is to join in with courage and patience and with each other.

Life, breath, food, companionship—every good thing is a gift from the abundant providence of God. The kingdom of God, this great economy, is embodied in the world when God's people respond to God's provision with gratitude, sharing God's gifts generously with others. The word *economy* reminds us again that creation is God's household; we are tasked with sustaining it and keeping it in the order God intended. It should be a place where all humans and all creatures are loved and honored and where generosity is commonplace.

As we close this book, we want to reemphasize that although the local community of believers is vital to our account of Slow Church, the story in which find ourselves is God's and not our own. Slow Church is not a utopian vision. The end we are bearing witness to is not the glorification of the church, but the glorification of God, without whom the church—and yes, even life itself—would not be possible.

There's a fine line between seeking the common *shalom* of creation as the faithful community of God's people and seeking what we, in our puny human wisdom, deem to be in the best interest of our own community. The Old Testament is full of stories of Israel careening back and forth from faithfulness to unfaithfulness. A basic church history textbook would feature more of the same. Our local gatherings can similarly be trusted to go off course as we seek our own will and desires—and then we are re-centered by a loving, astoundingly patient God. This wandering—and the struggle for us as a community of broken human beings to discern the direction God is leading us at any given time—is part of what makes Slow Church slow. The end of our story, however, must necessarily be the eternal kingdom of God, and not our own. This is why we pray, "Your kingdom come, your will be done, on earth as it is in heaven."

The fact that we are called to follow God in community is a hedge against the waywardness of our individual desires. The local church is the crucible in which our desires are transformed from the building of our individual and tribal kingdoms to the seeking of God's all-encompassing *shalom*. We hope that the language of Slow Church offers a contrast to a consumer Christianity that is driven by chasing after our own kingdoms.

Seeking to be the church well, as described in the first part of this book, stands in contrast to the temptations of power and prestige that come from measuring our faith by the standards of quantity instead of quality.

Recognizing that God's mission in the world is the reconciliation of all creation, as we explored in the second part of the book, stands in contrast to the temptation to be absorbed by the narrowness of our own individual or local kingdoms.

Finally, as we outlined in the third part of this book, the call to an economy of generous sharing—rooted in God's abundant provision for creation—stands in contrast to our temptation to greed and to hoarding resources in fear that we might not have enough.

The project of God's peculiar people has been underway since the fall of humankind in the Garden of Eden and will continue to unfold according to God's timetable. We've been formed by a culture of speed, but if we recognize our malformation, and the selfishness and fearfulness that are fueling it, perhaps we will become less resistant to God's transformation. Maybe we will taste, in a deeper way, the rich joys of God's kingdom.

Acknowledgments

One way to stay motivated during the slow work of writing a book about Slow Church is to think fondly about all the people you will get to thank in the acknowledgments. So thank you, all, for that too.

To David Zimmerman, Andrew Bronson, Adrianna Wright and the whole team at InterVarsity Press—thank you for faithfully shepherding us through this process, from proposal to publication.

To Patton Dodd, Deb Arca and the others at Patheos—thanks for giving us the opportunity to hammer out some of the ideas in this book on our blog, and for opening up the conversation about Slow Church to a broader internet audience.

FROM CHRIS

To John—thank you for the invitation to join you on the journey of writing this book. You are a true craftsman of words; this book is a much better one as a result of your mindful laboring over every word. I have learned volumes on the craft of writing from your example.

To Jeni, Alex, Miriam and Noah—thank you for your love and support throughout the book-writing process. And thank you especially for the weekends away that allowed me to make significant progress on early drafts of several chapters. Our adventures in living in community, as a family and as part of the churches to which we have belonged, were the fertile soil in which the ideas of this book took root in my mind. May we continue to grow deeper in the rich life of God's people!

To my Englewood family—I would not have been able to write this book without our life together. Thanks especially to my Sunday school class, who spent over a year reading and poring meticulously over every last word of this book. Your thoughtful critiques played a crucial role in revising and re-revising the manuscript. Thanks also to our Sunday night conversation group; you always stretch my imagination of what a church can become. I am indebted to Englewood Community Development Corp., my employer, for giving me the space and encouraging me to work on this book amidst my other responsibilities. And thanks to everyone else at Englewood whose conversation and witness remind me daily that Slow Church is not a far-fetched ideal, but a present reality into which we are ever stumbling together.

To my neighbors on the Near Eastside of Indianapolis—you have taught me what it means to belong to a place, and for that I am deeply grateful. You are a bold witness that diverse neighbors can work together for the health and well-being on their place.

To Jonathan Wilson-Hartgrove, Ragan Sutterfield and Phil Kenneson—thank you for taking time out of your busy schedule to read and provide substantial feedback on early chapter drafts. Your lives and your work are an inspiration and a hopeful witness that Slow Church is a possible and viable way of life.

To the Ekklesia Project—it was in your midst that I first heard the words *slow church,* almost a decade ago. Thank you for ever challenging the theological imaginations of God's people, and especially for convening a conversation in 2012 on Slow Church, a gathering that contributed significantly to the writing and revising of this book.

To Kara Faris and the Indiana Center for Congregations—thank you for the opportunity to refine some of the material here by presenting it to congregational leaders from across the state.

To Aaron Klinefelter and Charlie Brumbaugh and the good folks at the Episcopal Church of the Redeemer in Cincinnati—thank you for the opportunity to participate in your 2013 Lenten conversations on sabbath, which helped me flesh out several key parts of the book.

To David Neuhouser—thank you for immersing me as a college student in the work of Wendell Berry. Had you not done so, this book would likely never have come to fruition. Thank you for your continuing friendship and support over the last two decades.

And finally, to the readers of *The Englewood Review of Books*, thank you for your friendship and your continual engagement with us in wading through the endless stream of new books. Without you, I might never have read and been formed by many of the works that eventually gave shape to this book.

FROM JOHN

To Chris Smith—thank you for journeying together with me on this project. The first rule of cowriting a book is to work with a coauthor who is smarter than you are. I got that with you. Please extend my gratitude to your lovely family and to your neighbors in Englewood.

To Ryan Hamm and Roxanne Wieman, my editors at *Relevant* and *Neue* magazines, where some of this material first appeared—thank you for your care.

To my friends and colleagues at *Conspire* and the Burnside Writers Collective—for as long as I can remember, I've been driven by this vision of writers and artists coming together to make the world a better place. Thanks for letting me conspire with you all as we imagine alternatives to franchise faith.

To Paul Sparks, Tim Soerens, Dwight Friesen, Brandon Rhodes and the Parish Collective, and to my friends in the Leadership in the New Parish cohort—thank you for teaching me so much about what it means to weave a fabric of care in my neighborhood.

To my Portland and Chico friends, including the Family Dinner house churches, Matt and Grace, Mark and Alexis, Jordan and Mindy Green, Ramón Chaparro, the Nevenses, David and Kristialyn Johnson, and all the rest—thank you for your continued love and support.

To my neighbors in Silverton, with special thanks to Silverton Friends Church, the Upstream Makers Collective, Jack and Laurlyn

Long, Johna Rickard, the Ridgeways, and Bob and Sue Henry (and, of course, Alex, Sam and Lewis)—Kate and I committed to stay in Silverton for twenty years, but we love you all so much twenty years doesn't seem nearly long enough.

To the early readers of the manuscript, including Aimee, Eryn, Greg, Helen, Jim, Kevin, Lynette, Mark, Phil, Sally, Stanley and Tom—thank you for your thoughtful feedback.

To the Forum class—thank you for exploring with me what it means to create a safe place to have unsafe conversations.

To Kurt, Summer, Tyler and Wayne at Gear-Up Espresso—thank you for your hospitality.

To the guys at the Oak Street house: Ben, Waylan and especially John Friedrick—thank you for keeping me radical.

To my housemates, Mike, Lisa and John Leslie—you have been unbelievably kind and patient during the writing and editing of this book, giving me space when I needed space and ideas when I needed inspiration, not to mention encouragement and the occasional kick in the pants. What an interesting season of life we are in. I'm so happy to be sharing it with you.

To my parents, my brothers, my in-laws and to Libby Stokes—thank you for everything.

To Kate, Molly and Julia—what can I say? I can't imagine writing a book that isn't dedicated to you because, as any author will attest, book writing involves the whole family. You're the cowriters and the first readers; you help me think through ideas and wrestle words to the ground, and you inspire me to live up to my own ideals. Even when I was off at a coffee shop, or at the Abbey, or on retreat, I was always thinking about how this book was about you and for you. Thank you especially, Kate, for your patience, stability, abundance, hard work, delightfulness, gratitude, hospitality and commitment to conversation. You were embodying the values of Slow Church long before I started to write about them.

Recommended Reading

CHAPTER 1: A THEOLOGICAL VISION FOR SLOW CHURCH

Rodney Clapp, *A Peculiar People: The Church as Culture in a Post-Christian Society*

Gerhard Lohfink, *Jesus and Community*

Gerhard Lohfink, *Does God Need the Church? Toward a Theology of the People of God*

Samuel Wells, *Improvisation: The Drama of Christian Ethics*

EkklesiaProject.org

CHAPTER 2: *TERROIR*

Carlo Petrini, *Slow Food: The Case for Taste*

Carlo Petrini, *Slow Food Nation: Why Our Food Should Be Good, Clean, and Fair*

Lesslie Newbigin, *The Open Secret: An Introduction to the Theology of Mission*

John Drane, *The McDonaldization of the Church: Consumer Culture and the Church's Future*

Paul Sparks, Tim Soerens and Dwight J. Friesen, *The New Parish: How Neighborhood Churches Are Transforming Mission, Discipleship and Community*

John Drane, *After McDonaldization: Mission, Ministry, and Christian Discipleship in an Age of Uncertainty*

CHAPTER 3: STABILITY

Liberty Hyde Bailey, *Wind and Weather: Poems*

Andy Crouch, *Culture Making: Recovering Our Creative Calling*

Willie James Jennings, *The Christian Imagination: Theology and the Origins of Race*

Scott Russell Sanders, *Staying Put: Making a Home in a Restless World*

Jonathan Wilson-Hartgrove, *The Wisdom of Stability: Rooting Faith in a Mobile Culture*

Jonathan Wilson-Hartgrove, *The Rule of Saint Benedict: A Contemporary Paraphrase*

ParishCollective.org

CHAPTER 4: PATIENCE

Jacques Ellul, *The Technological Society*

Donald P. McNeill, Douglas A. Morrison and Henri Nouwen, *Compassion: A Reflection on the Christian Life*

Eugene Peterson, *The Jesus Way: A Conversation on the Ways That Jesus Is the Way*

Tertullian, *Of Patience*

CHAPTER 5: WHOLENESS

Bill Bishop, *The Big Sort: Why the Clustering of Like-Minded America Is Tearing Us Apart*

Madeleine L'Engle, *A Stone for a Pillow: Journeys with Jacob*

Robert Putnam, *Bowling Alone: The Collapse and Revival of American Community*

Chris Rice and Emmanuel Katongole, *Reconciling All Things: A Christian Vision for Justice, Peace and Healing*

Howard A. Snyder and Joel Scandrett, *Salvation Means Creation Healed: The Ecology of Sin and Grace*

CHAPTER 6: WORK

Matthew B. Crawford, *Shop Class as Soulcraft: An Inquiry into the Value of Work*

David H. Jensen, *Responsive Labor: A Theology of Work*

Richard Sennett, *The Corrosion of Character: The Personal Consequences of Work in the New Capitalism*

Amy Sherman, *Kingdom Calling: Vocational Stewardship for the Common Good*

Miroslav Volf, *Work in the Spirit: Toward a Theology of Work*

thehighcalling.org

CHAPTER 7: SABBATH

Dan Allender, *Sabbath*

Abraham Joshua Heschel, *The Sabbath*

Ched Myers, *The Biblical Vision of Sabbath Economics*

Judith Shulevitz, *The Sabbath World: Glimpses of a Different Order of Time*

Norman Wirzba, *Living the Sabbath: Discovering the Rhythms of Rest and Delight*

CHAPTER 8: ABUNDANCE

Mark Lau Branson, *Memories, Hopes, and Conversations: Appreciative Inquiry and Congregational Change*

William T. Cavanaugh, *Being Consumed: Economics and Christian Desire*

John McKnight and Peter Block, *The Abundant Community: Awakening the Power of Families and Neighborhoods*

Walter Brueggemann, "Sabbath as a Means of Transition from Anxious Scarcity to Grateful Abundance" (talk given at Eastern Mennonite University, January 2012, emu.edu/now/podcast/2012/01/18/"sabbath-as-a-means-of-transition-from-anxious-scarcity-to-grateful-abundance"-dr-walter-Brueggemann

Asset-Based Community Development Institute, abcdinstitute.org

CHAPTER 9: GRATITUDE

Peter Block, *Community: The Structure of Belonging*

John P. Kretzmann and John L. McKnight, *Building Communities from the Inside Out*

Mary Jo Leddy, *Radical Gratitude*

John McKnight and Peter Block, *The Abundant Community: Awakening the Power of Families and Neighborhoods*

Christine D. Pohl, *Living into Community: Cultivating Practices That Sustain Us*

Luther K. Snow, *The Power of Asset Mapping: How Your Congregation Can Act on Its Gifts*

CHAPTER 10: HOSPITALITY

Elizabeth Newman, *Untamed Hospitality: Welcoming God and Other Strangers*
Henri J. M. Nouwen, *Reaching Out: The Three Movements of the Spiritual Life*
Amy G. Oden (ed.), *And You Welcomed Me: A Sourcebook on Hospitality in Early Christianity*
Christine D. Pohl, *Making Room: Recovering Hospitality as a Christian Tradition*
Arthur Sutherland, *I Was a Stranger: A Christian Theology of Hospitality*

CHAPTER 11: DINNER TABLE CONVERSATION AS A WAY OF BEING CHURCH

Norman Wirzba, *Food and Faith: A Theology of Eating*
John Backman, *Why Can't We Talk? Christian Wisdom on Dialogue as a Habit of the Heart*
C. Christopher Smith, *The Virtue of Dialogue: Conversation as a Hopeful Practice of Church Communities*
Miriam Weinstein, *The Surprising Power of Family Meals: How Eating Together Makes Us Smarter, Stronger, Healthier, and Happier*
Alan J. Roxburgh, *Missional: Joining God in the Neighborhood*

Notes

INTRODUCTION

[1]F. T. Marinetti played his part. He enthusiastically supported Italy's entry into World War I, staging fights with other Futurists as pro-war demonstrations. He created the Futurist Political Party in 1918 and supported Benito Mussolini's rise to power. In his late fifties, Marinetti volunteered to fight in the war that resulted in the Italian colonization of Ethiopia, and during World War II, when Marinetti was in his sixties, he volunteered to serve on the Russian front.

[2]Carlo Petrini, *Slow Food: The Case for Taste* (New York: Columbia University Press, 2001), p. xxiii.

[3]Carl Honoré, *In Praise of Slowness: Challenging the Cult of Speed* (New York: HarperOne, 2004), pp. 14-15.

[4]George Ritzer, *The McDonaldization of Society,* 20th Anniversary ed. (Thousand Oaks, CA: Sage, 2013), p. 1.

[5]Joel Salatin, *You Can Farm: The Entrepreneur's Guide to Start and Succeed in a Farming Enterprise* (Swoope, VA: Polyface, 1998).

[6]See Gus Frederick, *Silverton,* Images of America (Charleston, SC: Arcadia, 2011).

[7]For more on this, see Jack Hitt, *Bunch of Amateurs: A Search for the American Character* (New York: Crown Publishing, 2012).

[8]Wendell Berry, "The Pleasures of Eating," in *What Are People For?* (New York: Farrar, Straus & Giroux, 1990), p. 145.

CHAPTER 1: A THEOLOGICAL VISION FOR SLOW CHURCH

[1]Kevin J. Vanhoozer, *The Drama of Doctrine: A Canonical Linguistic Approach to Christian Doctrine* (Lexington, KY: Westminster John Knox Press, 2005), pp. 37-38.

[2]Tina Fey, *Bossypants* (New York: Back Bay Books, 2012), pp. 84-85.

[3]N. T. Wright, *Scripture and the Authority of God: How to Read the Bible Today* (San Francisco: HarperOne, 2011), p. 123.

[4]Samuel Wells, *Improvisation: The Drama of Christian Ethics* (Grand Rapids: Brazos, 2004), p. 11.

[5]Quoted in Robert Inchausti, *Subversive Orthodoxy: Outlaws, Revolutionaries, and Other Christians in Disguise* (Grand Rapids: Brazos, 2005), p. 9.

[6]Ibid., p. 11.

[7]Gerhard Lohfink, *Does God Need the Church? Toward a Theology of the People of God,* trans. Linda M. Maroney (Collegeville, MN: Liturgical Press, 1999), p. 48, emphasis added.

[8]John Milton, *Paradise Lost,* book IV.

[9]Quoted in John C. Nugent, *The Politics of Yahweh: John Howard Yoder, the Old Testament, and the People of God* (Eugene, OR: Wipf & Stock, 2011), pp. 30-31.

[10]Lohfink, *Does God Need the Church?* p. 174.

[11]Ibid., p. 220, emphasis in original.

[12]Ibid., pp. 223-24.

[13]Michael Frost and Alan Hirsch, *The Shaping of Things to Come: Innovation and Mission for the 21st-Century Church* (Peabody, MA: Hendrickson, 2003), p. 225.

[14]Ibid., p. 12.

[15]Ibid., p. 47.

[16]Wendell Berry, *That Distant Land: The Collected Stories of Wendell Berry* (Berkeley, CA: Counterpoint, 2004), p. 356.

CHAPTER 2: *TERROIR*

[1]James Twitchell, *Shopping for God: How Christianity Went from in Your Heart to in Your Face* (New York: Simon & Schuster, 2007), p. 254.

[2]See Michael Pollan, *The Omnivore's Dilemma: A Natural History of Four Meals* (New York: Penguin, 2006), pp. 117-18.

[3]Carlo Petrini, *Slow Food: The Case for Taste* (New York: Columbia University Press, 2001), p. 8.

[4]Alan J. Roxburgh, *Missional: Joining God in the Neighborhood* (Grand Rapids: Baker Books, 2011), p. 133.

[5]Ibid., p. 148.

[6]From "Reimagining the Parish," a conversation between Paul Sparks and Chris Smith. Audio available at http://erb.kingdomnow.org/paul-sparks-chris-smith-reimagining-the-parish-audio.

[7]See C. Peter Wagner's introduction to Donald A. McGavran's *Understanding Church Growth*, 3rd ed. (Grand Rapids: Eerdmans, 1990).

[8]McGavran, *Understanding Church Growth*, p. ix.

[9]Gary L. McIntosh, "Church Movements of the Last Fifty Years in the USA: Four Major Church Movements." Available at: http://churchgrowthnetwork. com/free-resources/2010/08/20/church-movements-of-the-last-fifty-years-in-the-usa.

[10]McGavran, *Understanding Church Growth*, p. 225.

[11]Ibid., p. 163.

[12]Ralph H. Elliott, "Dangers of the Church Growth Movement," *Christian Century*, August 12-19, 1981. Available online at www.religion-online.org/showarticle.asp?title=1723.

[13]Donald McGavran, *The Bridges of God* (New York: Friendship Press, 1968), pp. 44, 59.

[14]Alan Hirsch, *Forgotten Ways: Reactivating the Missional Church* (Grand Rapids: Brazos, 2006), pp. 44-45.

[15]McGavran, *Understanding Church Growth*, p. 67.

[16]See Lesslie Newbigin, *The Open Secret: An Introduction to the Theology of Mission* (Grand Rapids: Eerdmans, 1995), pp. 124-26.

[17]Bob DeWaay, "Faulty Premises of the Church Growth Movement: Rick Warren, Robert Schuller, Donald McGavran, and C. Peter Wagner Mislead the Church." Available at http://cicministry.org/commentary/issue89.htm.

[18]Hirsch, *Forgotten Ways*, p. 45.

[19]Ritzer, *McDonaldization of Society*, p. 87.

[20]John Drane, *The McDonaldization of the Church: Consumer Culture and the Church's Future* (Macon, GA: Smith & Helwys, 2001), pp. 50-51.

[21]Ritzer, *McDonaldization of Society*, p. 102.

[22]Drane, *McDonaldization of the Church*, p. 51.

[23]Quoted in Elliot, "Dangers of the Church Growth Movement."

[24]Ibid.

[25]Drane, *McDonaldization of the Church*, pp. 52-53.

[26]Brother David Steindle-Rast, *A Listening Heart* (New York: Crossroad, 1999), p. 78.

CHAPTER 3: STABILITY

[1]George A. Smith, *The Apple Tree Community* (Great Neck, NY: Channel Press, 1960), p. 5.

[2]Robert J. Banks, *Paul's Idea of Community: The Early House Churches in Their Cultural Setting*, rev. ed. (Grand Rapids: Baker Academic, 2012), p. 42.

[3]According to a recent National Highway Traffic Safety Administration report, 4,280 pedestrians were killed (the equivalent of one death every two hours) and 70,000 pedestrians were injured in motor vehicle traffic crashes in 2010. That same year, 618 cyclists were killed and 52,000 cyclists were injured in traffic crashes.

[4]Willie James Jennings, *The Christian Imagination: Theology and the Origins of Race* (New Haven, CT: Yale University Press, 2011), p. 293.

[5]See Bill Bishop, *The Big Sort: Why the Clustering of Like-Minded America is Tearing Us Apart* (New York: Houghton Mifflin, 2008).

[6]Wendell Berry, *Jayber Crow* (Washington, DC: Counterpoint, 2000), p. 298; Wendell Berry, "Sabbaths 2007, No. VI," in *Leavings* (Berkeley, CA: Counterpoint, 2010), p. 91.

[7]Parker J. Palmer, *To Know as We Are Known: Education as a Spiritual Journey* (New York: HarperCollins, 1993), pp. 8-9.

[8]Andy Crouch, *Culture Making: Recovering Our Creative Calling* (Downers Grove, IL: InterVarsity Press, 2008), pp. 75-76.

[9]The word "cultureshed" was coined by Jay Salinas of The Wormfarm Institute. He defines it this way: "Cultureshed: n. 1. A geographic region irrigated by streams of local talent and fed by deep pools of human and natural history. 2. An area nourished by what is cultivated locally. 3. The efforts of writers, performers, visual artists, scholars, farmers and chefs who contribute to a vital and diverse local culture" (www.wormfarminstitute.org).

CHAPTER 4: PATIENCE

[1]Henri Nouwen, Donald P. McNeill and Douglas A. Morrison, *Compassion: A Reflection on the Christian Life* (New York: Image Books, 1983), p. 94.

[2]Nicholas Wolterstorff, *Lament for a Son* (Grand Rapids: Eerdmans, 1987), pp. 72-73.

[3]Phil Kennson. "Practicing Ekklesial Patience," *Ekklesia Project Pamplet* 20 (2013): 16.

[4]Nouwen, McNeill and Morrison, *Compassion,* pp. 90-91.

⁵C. Christopher Smith, *Water, Faith and Wood: Stories of the Early Church's Witness for Today* (Indianapolis: Doulos Christou Press, 2003), p. 149.

⁶Philip D. Kenneson, Practicing Ecclesial Patience: Patient Practice Makes Perfect (Eugene, OR: Wipf & Stock, 2013), pp. 23-24. Available online at www.ekklesiaproject.org/wp-content/uploads/2011/05.

⁷William T. Cavanaugh, *Being Consumed: Economics and Christian Desire* (Grand Rapids: Eerdmans, 2008), p. 58.

⁸Eugene Peterson, *The Jesus Way: A Conversation on the Ways That Jesus Is the Way* (Grand Rapids: Eerdmans, 2007), p. 7.

⁹Ibid., p. 4.

CHAPTER 5: WHOLENESS

¹Roddy Scheer and Doug Moss, "United States Leads the World in Consuming Natural Resources," *E Magazine,* September 9, 2012. Available online at www .emagazine.com/earth-talk/united-states-leads-in-consuming-natural-resources.

²Nancy Mathis, *Storm Warning: The Story of a Killer Tornado* (New York: Touchstone, 2007), p. x.

³Howard A. Snyder with Joel Scandrett, *Salvation Means Creation Healed: The Ecology of Sin and Grace* (Eugene, OR: Cascade Books, 2011), p. xvi.

⁴Rollins calls these fragmentations "sins of abstraction," meaning that by focusing intently on such a narrow focus we are, in essence, abstracting that area of focus out of the whole.

⁵"Pastor Rick Warren Born Again to Healthier Living," *USA Today,* February 6, 2012. Available online at http://yourlife.usatoday.com/fitness-food/diet-nutrition/story/2012-02-05/Pastor-Rick-Warren-born-again-to-healthier-living/52975790/1.

⁶Wendy Ryan, "Baptist Leaders' 'Berlin Declaration' Challenges 'Racial and Ethnic Hatred,'" *Baptist Press,* June 5, 2001. Available online at www.bpnews .net/bpnews.asp?ID=11040.

⁷John Howard Yoder, "Church Growth Issues in Theological Perspective," in *The Challenge of Church Growth: A Symposium,* ed. Wilbert R. Shenk, Institute of Mennonite Studies (Scottdale, PA: Herald Press, 1973), p. 29.

⁸Alan Hirsch, *The Forgotten Ways: Reactivating the Missional Church* (Grand Rapids: Brazos, 2006), p. 45.

⁹Bill Bishop, *The Big Sort: Why the Clustering of Like-Minded America Is Tearing Us Apart* (New York: Mariner Books, 2008), pp. 297-98.

[10]"Seeking Unity on Election Day," *The Lima (OH) News*, November 2012. Available online at http://m.limaohio.com/lifestyle/religion/article_3597b522-249e-11e2-b124-0019bb30f31a.html.

[11]Andrew Marin, *Love Is an Orientation: Elevating the Conversation with the Gay Community* (Downers Grove, IL: InterVarsity Press, 2009), p. 187.

[12]See www.lasallestreetchurch.org.

[13]Thomas Merton, *New Seeds of Contemplation* (New York: New Directions, 1961), p. 122.

[14]Wendell Berry, "The Wages of History," in *Farming: A Hand Book* (Berkeley, CA: Counterpoint, 2011), p. 113.

[15]Parker J. Palmer, "The Clearness Committee: A Communal Approach to Discernment." Available online at www.couragerenewal.org/parker/writings/clearness-committee. See also Palmer, *A Hidden Wholeness: The Journey Toward an Undivided Life* (San Francisco: Jossey-Bass, 2009).

[16]Palmer, "Clearness Committee."

[17]Lesli J. Favor, *The Iroquois Constitution: A Primary Source Investigation of the Law of the Iroquois* (New York: Rosen, 2003), p. 99.

CHAPTER 6: WORK

[1]See Ray Oldenburg, *The Great Good Place: Cafés, Coffee Shops, Bookstores, Bars, Hair Salons, and Other Hangouts at the Heart of a Community* (New York: Marlowe, 1999), and *Celebrating the Third Place: Inspiring Stories About the "Great Good Places" at the Heart of Our Communities* (New York: Marlowe, 2001).

[2]David Fitch, "'You Go to McDonald's Too Much!' On Being Called Out and the 'politics of the small things,'" *Reclaiming the Mission* (blog), February 2, 2012, www.reclaimingthemission.com/?p=2749.

[3]Studs Terkel, *Working: People Talk About What They Do All Day and How They Feel About What They Do* (New York: New Press, 1974), p. xi.

[4]G. K. Chesterton, *What's Wrong with the World* (New York: Dodd, Mead, 1910).

[5]M. Douglas Meeks, *God the Economist* (Minneapolis: Fortress, 2000), p. 137.

[6]Quoted in ibid., p. 33.

[7]Miroslav Volf, *Work in the Spirit: Toward a Theology of Work* (Oxford: Oxford University Press, 1991), p. 145.

[8]We'd like to acknowledge from the start Volf's *Work in the Spirit*, which has

been enormously helpful as we've tried to think theologically about Adam Smith, Karl Marx, capitalism, the division of labor, alienation and so on.

[9]Ibid., p. 157.

[10]Adam Smith, *The Wealth of Nations* (New York: Bantam Books, 2003), p. 987.

[11]George Ritzer, *The McDonaldization of Society*, 20th Anniversary ed. (Thousand Oaks, CA: Sage, 2013), p. 35.

[12]Ibid., p. 108.

[13]Matthew B. Crawford, *Shop Class as Soulcraft: An Inquiry into the Value of Work* (New York: Penguin, 2009), p. 37.

[14]Ibid., pp. 41-42.

[15]Ritzer, *McDonaldization of Society*, p. 102.

[16]Quoted in Laura K. Simmons, *Creed Without Chaos: Exploring Theology in the Writings of Dorothy Sayers* (Grand Rapids: Baker Academic, 2005), pp. 117-18.

[17]David H. Jensen says in *Responsive Labor: A Theology of Work* that the main distinction between work and worship is that work is not the chief end of human beings, that Christian worship sets limits to human work, and that "work is for the sake of communion, not communion for the sake of work" ([Louisville: Westminster John Knox, 2006], pp. 68-70).

[18]Kathleen Norris, *The Quotidian Mysteries: Laundry, Liturgy, and "Women's Work"* (Mahwah, NJ: Paulist Press, 1998), p. 22.

[19]The source for these statistics, and more information about child labor, can be found at the website of the UN's World Day Against Child Labour (www.un.org/en/events/childlabourday), as well as at the International Labour Organization (www.ilo.org), Anti-Slavery International (www.antislavery.org) and Compassion International (www.compassion.com/children-and-poverty.htm).

[20]Mark Scandrette, *Practicing the Way of Jesus: Life Together in the Kingdom of Love* (Downers Grove, IL: InterVarsity Press, 2011).

CHAPTER 7: SABBATH

[1]See Dan Gibson, Jordan Green and John Pattison, *Besides the Bible: 100 Books That Have, Should, or Will Create Christian Culture* (Downers Grove, IL: InterVarsity Press, 2010), p. 17.

[2]Peter J. Thuesen, *Predestination: The American Career of a Contentious Doctrine* (New York: Oxford University Press, 2009), p. 58.

[3]Josef Pieper, *Leisure: The Basis of Culture* (New York: Random House, 1963), p. 20.

[4]Mark Kelly, "LifeWay Research Finds Pastors' Long Work Hours Come at Expense of People, Ministry," January 5, 2010, www.lifeway.com/Article/ LifeWay-Research-finds-pastors-long-work-hours-can-come-at-the-expense-of-people-ministry.

[5]Thomas Merton, *Conjectures of a Guilty Bystander* (New York: Doubleday, 1965), p. 81.

[6]Richard H. Lowery, *Sabbath and Jubilee* (St. Louis, MO: Chalice Press, 2000), p. 3.

[7]Ched Myers, *The Biblical Vision of Sabbath Economics* (Washington, DC: Tell the Word Press, 2001), p. 12.

[8]Quoted in Myers, *Biblical Vision of Sabbath Economics,* p. 13.

[9]Pope John Paul II, "Dies Domini: An Apostolic Letter of the Holy Father to the Bishops, Clergy and Faithful of the Catholic Church on Keeping the Lord's Day Holy," July 5, 1998. Available online at www.vatican.va/holy_father/john_paul_ii/apost_letters/documents/hf_jp_ii_apl_05071998_dies-domini_en.html.

[10]From a Midrash by Rashi on Megillah 9a, quoted in *The Sabbath*, by Abraham Joshua Heschel (New York: Farrar, Straus & Giroux, 1951), p. 22.

[11]Dan Allender, *Sabbath* (Nashville: Thomas Nelson, 2009), p. 28.

[12]Norman Wirzba, *Living the Sabbath: Discovering the Rhythms of Rest and Delight* (Grand Rapids: Brazos Press, 2006), pp. 33-34.

[13]Allender, *Sabbath,* p. 25.

[14]Judith Shulevitz, *The Sabbath World: Glimpses of a Different Order of Time* (New York: Random House, 2011), p. 5.

[15]Wirzba, *Living the Sabbath,* p. 57, emphasis in original.

[16]Ibid., p. 59.

CHAPTER 8: ABUNDANCE

[1]Gerhard Lohfink, *Does God Need the Church? Toward a Theology of the People of God,* trans. Linda M. Maloney (Collegeville, MN: Liturgical Press, 1999), p. 149.

[2]Roger E. Backhouse and Steven Medema, "Retrospectives: On the Definition of Economics," *Journal of Economic Perspectives* 23, no. 1 (2009): 225, emphasis added.

[3]"Six Questions on the Cost of Corruption with World Bank Institute Global Governance Director Daniel Kaufmann," available at http://go.worldbank.org/KQH743GKF1.

[4]Wendell Berry, *A Continuous Harmony: Essays Cultural and Agricultural* (Berkeley, CA: Counterpoint, 2012), p. 116.

[5]Ibid., pp. 116-17.

[6]William T. Cavanaugh, *Being Consumed: Economics and Christian Desire* (Grand Rapids: Eerdmans, 2008), p. 90.

[7]Ibid., p. 91.

[8]Ibid., p. 92.

[9]"The Economy's Impact on Churches (Part 2 of 3): How Churches Have Adapted," January 25, 2010. Available at www.barna.org/barna-update/article/18-congregations/334-the-economys-impact-on-churches-part-2-of-3-how-churches-have-adapted.

[10]Luther Snow, *The Power of Asset Mapping: How Your Congregation Can Act on Its Gifts* (Herndon, VA: Alban Institute, 2004), pp. 119-20.

[11]Walter Brueggemann. "The Liturgy of Abundance, the Myth of Scarcity" *The Christian Century,* March 24-31, 1999. Accessed online at www.religion-online.org/showarticle.asp?title=533.

[12]Ibid.

[13]Ibid.

[14]Lohfink, *Does God Need the Church?* p. 146.

[15]Ibid., pp. 144-45.

[16]In the ELCA, for instance, churches in urban places were much more likely to close than in rural or suburban places, and "churches were three times more likely to close when they were in communities where less than 75% of the population was white," a demographic that is primarily true of urban neighborhoods (David Olson, *The American Church in Crisis* [Grand Rapids: Zondervan, 2008], pp. 121-22).

[17]Wendell Berry. "Sabbath Poems 2007, No. VI," in *Leavings* (Berkeley, CA: Counterpoint, 2010), p. 91.

CHAPTER 9: GRATITUDE

[1]Royce G. Gruenler, *The Trinity in the Gospel of John* (Grand Rapids: Baker, 1986), p. 121.

[2]Christine D. Pohl, *Living into Community: Cultivating Practices That Sustain Us* (Grand Rapids: Eerdmans, 2011), p. 23.

[3]David W. Pao, *Thanksgiving: An Investigation of a Pauline Theme*, New Studies in Biblical Theology (Downers Grove, IL: InterVarsity Press, 2002), p. 15.

[4]Pohl, *Living into Community*, p. 17.

[5]Ibid., p. 23.

[6]Gus Lubin, "There's a Staggering Conspiracy Behind the Rise of Consumer Culture," *Business Insider*, February 23, 2013, www.businessinsider.com/birth-of-consumer-culture-2013-2?op=1.

[7]Mary Jo Leddy, *Radical Gratitude* (Maryknoll, NY: Orbis, 2002), p. 57.

[8]Ibid., p. 7.

[9]See ibid., p. 4.

[10]Quoted in Pohl, *Living into Community*, p. 22.

[11]Dietrich Bonhoeffer, *Life Together: The Classic Exploration of Faith in Community* (New York: HarperCollins, 1954), pp. 27-28.

[12]Luther K. Snow, *The Power of Asset Mapping: How Your Congregation Can Act on Its Gifts* (Herndon, VA: Alban Institute, 2004), p. 5. Snow adapted this list from the work of John P. Kretzmann and John L. McKnight, *Building Communities from the Inside Out* (Evanston, IL: ABCD Institute, 1993).

[13]Mark Lau Branson, *Memories, Hopes and Conversations: Appreciative Inquiry and Congregational Change* (Herndon, VA: Alban Institute, 2004), p. xiii.

[14]Ibid., p. 28.

[15]Ibid., p. 2.

[16]Ibid., p. 124.

[17]Kretzmann and McKnight, *Building Communities from the Inside Out*, pp. 4-5.

[18]Ibid., p. 9.

[19]Pohl, *Living into Community*, p. 23.

[20]Ibid., pp. 29-30.

[21]Ibid., p. 53.

[22]Questions 2 and 3 here have been adapted from Branson's *Memories, Hopes and Conversations*, pp. 146-47.

CHAPTER 10: HOSPITALITY

[1]Kathryn Spink, *The Miracle, the Message, the Story: Jean Vanier and L'Arche* (Mahwah, NJ: Hidden Spring, 2006), p. 57.

[2]Jean Vanier, *Befriending the Stranger* (Mahwah, NJ: Paulist Press, 2010), p. 12, emphasis added.

[3]Christine D. Pohl, *Making Room: Recovering Hospitality as a Christian Tradition* (Grand Rapids: Eerdmans, 1999), p. 105.

[4]Ibid., p. 28.

[5]Bishop Yvette A. Flunder, a UCC minister and author of *Where the Edge Gathers: Building a Community of Radical Inclusion* (Cleveland, OH: Pilgrim, 2005), made this point during a talk at Wild Goose Festival (Corvallis, OR) in July 2012.

[6]For more on Clement of Alexandria, Lactantius, St. Gregory of Nyssa, St. Benedict and St. John the Almsgiver, see Amy G. Oden, *And You Welcomed Me: A Sourcebook on Hospitality in Early Christianity* (Nashville: Abingdon, 2001), pp. 50-85.

[7]Quoted in Pohl, *Making Room*, pp. 43-44.

[8]Ibid., p. 30.

[9]Kristine Thomas, "Shared Belief: Community Dinners, Distinguished Service," February 2012, Our Town, http://ourtownlive.com/ourtown/?p =2149.

[10]Henri J. M. Nouwen, *Reaching Out: The Three Movements of the Spiritual Life* (New York: Doubleday, 1975), p. 67.

[11]Elizabeth Newman, *Untamed Hospitality: Welcoming God and Other Strangers* (Grand Rapids: Brazos, 2007), p. 92.

[12]John Koenig, *New Testament Hospitality: Partnership with Strangers as Promise and Mission* (Eugene, OR: Wipf & Stock, 2001), p. 5.

[13]Newman, *Untamed Hospitality,* p. 91.

[14]Edward Relph, *Place and Placelessness* (London: Pion, 1976), preface.

[15]Ibid., p. 143.

[16]Arthur Sutherland, *I Was a Stranger: A Christian Theology of Hospitality* (Nashville: Abingdon, 2006), pp. 41, 43. See also Robert Banks, *Paul's Idea of Community*, Robert and Julia Banks, *The Church Comes Home* (Peabody, MA: Hendrickson, 1998), and John H. Elliott, *A Home for the Homeless* (Eugene, OR: Wipf & Stock, 2005), among others.

CHAPTER 11: DINNER TABLE CONVERSATION AS A WAY OF BEING THE CHURCH

[1]Eugene Peterson, *Reversed Thunder: The Revelation of John and the Praying Imagination* (San Francisco: Harper, 1991), p. 119.

[2]Dan Merica, "Washington Gridlock Linked to Social Funk," *CNN.com,* January 25, 2013, www.cnn.com/2013/01/25/politics/social-congress.

[3]Ibid.

[4]Fred Rogers, *The Mr. Rogers Parenting Book* (Philadelphia: Running Press, 2002), p. 19.

[5]Michael Pollan, *Cooked: A Natural History of Transformation* (New York: Penguin, 2013), p. 8.

[6]J. H. Yoder, *Body Politics* (Scottdale, PA: Herald Press, 2001), p. 16, emphasis in original.

[7]Ibid., p. 19.

[8]Norman Wirzba, *Food and Faith: A Theology of Eating* (New York: Cambridge University Press, 2011), p. 160.

[9]Rachel Marie Stone. *Eat with Joy: Redeeming God's Gift of Food* (Downers Grove, IL: InterVarsity Press, 2013), p. 69.

[10]Alan J. Roxburgh, *Missional: Joining God in the Neighborhood* (Grand Rapids: Baker, 2011), p. 145.

[11]Richard J. Foster, *Celebration of Discipline: The Path to Spiritual Growth* (San Francisco: HarperCollins, 1998), p. 182.

[12]Parker Palmer, "Good Teaching: A Matter of Living the Mystery," *Change* magazine, January/February 1990, www.couragerenewal.org/parker/writings/good-teaching.

[13]Tim Conder and Daniel Rhodes, *Free for All: Rediscovering the Bible in Community* (Grand Rapids: Baker, 2009), p. 85.

[14]Yoder, *Body Politics*, p. 17.

CONCLUSION

[1]Liberty Hyde Bailey, "Poet," in *Wind and Weather: Poems* (New York: Macmillan, 1916), p. 153.

God has called us to ministry. But it's not enough to have a vision for ministry if you don't have the practical skills for it. Nor is it enough to do the work of ministry if what you do is headed in the wrong direction. We need both vision *and* expertise for effective ministry. We need *praxis*.

Praxis puts theory into practice. It brings cutting-edge ministry expertise from visionary practitioners. You'll find sound biblical and theological foundations for ministry in the real world, with concrete examples for effective action and pastoral ministry. Praxis books are more than the "how to" – they're also the "why to." And because *being* is every bit as important as *doing*, Praxis attends to the inner life of the leader as well as the outer work of ministry. Feed your soul, and feed your ministry.

If you are called to ministry, you know you can't do it on your own. Let Praxis provide the companions you need to equip God's people for life in the kingdom.

www.ivpress.com/praxis